Richard L. Rohrbaugh

Jesus After the Gospels

Other books by Robert M. Grant
published by Westminster/John Knox Press

Greek Apologists of the Second Century

Gods and the One God
   (Library of Early Christianity)

JESUS AFTER THE GOSPELS

The Christ of the Second Century

Robert M. Grant

The Hale Memorial Lectures of Seabury-Western Theological Seminary 1989

Westminster/John Knox Press
Louisville, Kentucky

Scripture quotations are adapted from the Revised Standard Version of the Bible, copyrighted 1946, 1952, © 1971, 1973 by the Division of Christian Education of the National Council of the Churches of Christ in the U.S.A. and used by permission.

The Hale Lectures were established in 1900 under the terms of the will of the Right Reverend Charles Reuben Hale, D.D., LL.D., Bishop Coadjutor of Springfield, Illinois. He was born in 1837, consecrated on July 26, 1892, and died on December 25, 1900.

Book design by Gene Harris

First edition

Published by Westminster/John Knox Press
Louisville, Kentucky

PRINTED IN THE UNITED STATES OF AMERICA

9 8 7 6 5 4 3 2 1

Library of Congress Cataloging-in-Publication Data

Grant, Robert McQueen, 1917–
  Jesus after the Gospels : the Christ of the second century /
Robert M. Grant. — 1st ed.
      p.   cm.
  "The Hale memorial lectures of Seabury-Western Theological
Seminary, 1989."
  Includes bibliographical references.
  ISBN 0-664-21919-5

  1. Jesus Christ—History of doctrines—Early church, ca. 30–600.
I. Title. II. Title: Hale memorial lectures of Seabury-Western
Theological Seminary.
BT198.G715   1990
232'.09'.015—dc20   89-29057
                                                                  CIP

Contents

Preface

Sixty years ago when my father delivered the Hale Lectures for the Western Theological Seminary, he must have given them at Northwestern or Garrett since our elegant buildings had not yet been built. Two years later I heard some of the next series, given by my godfather, Burton Easton, on "Christ in the Gospels." The early years of Seabury-Western brought John Rathbone Oliver to speak of psychiatry and I heard all of Winfred Douglas' "Church Music in History and Practice," especially his memorable records of Spanish plainsong. Fifty years ago I went to Fleming James' famous lectures on "Personalities of the Old Testament." To round out this exercise in nostalgia: I taught at Seabury thirty-five years ago, while a mere twenty years ago I was given the D.D. on the occasion of my father's last visit to the seminary.

My father's 1928 topic was "New Horizons of the Christian Faith," an optimistic and forward-looking title that reflected American hopes just before the Depression as well as the new horizons of the Western Seminary, just then arriving in Evanston. My own lectures are optimistic in another way, for they point to an era of theological freedom and ferment that flourished when the early churches were seeking to express their faith in innovative, meaningful terms. They could have been entitled "Old Horizons of the Christian Faith."

The more adventurous New Testament authors did not keep their successors from thinking but left the way open for new forms of expression in new contexts. (Origen made a similar point in his preface to *First Principles*.) This opens up a basic reason for the study of the early fathers—to gain what Tillich called "the courage to be," to free ourselves from the belief that either Nicaea or Chalcedon was predestined. We have to imagine that we too are reworking diversified revelations, hoping to overcome some contradictions while retaining others for their paradoxical boldness.

The lectures deal with doctrines of the Christ, first with various biblical ideas, second with Gnostic Christologies, third with an influential Jewish Christian bishop and apologist, and fourth with the Christology of Irenaeus, Catholic but still boldly speculative. The goal is to show how some Gnostics and apologists, as well as a great anti-Gnostic theologian, could work out distinctive doctrines from the biblical materials.

I shall not emphasize the chronological and historical framework too much because I may have overemphasized such a framework for Gnosticism in my lectures of 1958 for the American Council of Learned Societies. In the case of Gnosticism, I now think that simple chronological succession does not prove a great deal about origins. There is also a temptation to lay excessive emphasis on one causal factor or only a few of them.

Even so, some historical correlations remain striking. First, Christology in the New Testament was chiefly developed during the period of creative tension before the Jewish revolt of A.D. 66–70; John's negative attitude toward "the Jews" as a group probably arose later. Second, Ignatius may reflect incipient conflicts at Antioch around the time of the Jewish revolt in 115–17, while the major early Gnostics, one of them at Antioch, certainly came to the fore along with another Jewish revolt in 132–35. After that there was a period of relative tranquillity from which come the materials used by the apologist Justin. It ended with the persecution of some Christians, but not Jews, around 177, and soon thereafter we find Theophilus writing a highly "Jewish" apology at Antioch. He reflects closeness between Jews and Christians, and his successor as bishop had to write against those who "fell from faith in

Christ to Jewish pseudo-worship at the time of the persecution"[1]: that is, escaped persecution by becoming Jews. Finally, when circumstances for Christians became better under Commodus, Irenaeus produced a balanced theology, though since he was human he tended to be quirky. The doctrinal developments cannot, however, be explained simply as the results of historical events or political circumstances. We have to allow for the development of logical and theological thinking as well as for the personalities of the various writers involved.

They reached no solutions with direct "relevance" for twentieth- or twenty-first-century theology, but they stated perennial problems in fresh ways that only later became classical and offered possible moves toward dealing with them. Later Christians need to review their exegetical search in order to continue it.

As Anglicans would expect, most of the authors to be discussed were concerned with balancing scripture and tradition with philosophical reason. One could even imagine Theophilus as a forerunner of some of the more venturesome Anglican bishops of the early twentieth century.

Perhaps I favor Irenaeus partly because Philip Carrington, Archbishop of Quebec, long ago taught me to view Irenaeus as his own predecessor.[2] I first met him on the old *Duchess of Athol* in 1930, and he first visited Western in 1933. In later decades his letters about the second century combined sober sense with fascinating speculation, and they reminded me of Irenaeus himself.

R.M.G.

Chicago 1989

The Hale Lectures
of Seabury-Western
Theological Seminary

1908   Peter C. Lutkin, *Music in the Church*

1910   John Wordsworth, *The National Church of Sweden*

1913   Anthony Mitchell, *Biographical Studies in Scottish Church History*

1914   Samuel A. B. Mercer, *The Ethiopic Liturgy: Its Sources, Development, and Present Form*

1922   Frank Gavin, *Some Aspects of Contemporary Greek Orthodox Thought*

1928   Frederick C. Grant, *New Horizons of the Christian Faith*

1930   Burton Scott Easton, *Christ in the Gospels*

1932   John Rathbone Oliver, *Pastoral Psychiatry and Mental Health*

1933   William George Peck, *The Social Implications of the Oxford Movement*

1935   Winfred Douglas, *Church Music in History and Practice: Studies in the Praise of God*

1937   Henry St. George Tucker, *The History of the Episcopal Church in Japan*

1938   Fleming James, *Personalities of the Old Testament*

1943   E. Clowes Chorley, *Men and Movements in the American Episcopal Church*

1946   Frank Arthur McElwain, *The Permanent Element in Old Testament Prophecy*

1
Biblical Christology: The Humanity of Christ

To say "Christology" is to say "Christ": that is, the human being who would be the expected Messiah or "anointed one" of Jewish hope, the one whom God "anointed" for a role like that of Old Testament kings, priests, and even prophets.

Around the time of Jesus, Jews had been ruled by foreigners like Pompey or Herod the Great or the Roman prefects for less than a century, and many hoped for the restoration of Israel as an independent kingdom, with its center at Jerusalem, the city of David. They inevitably pictured a coming king or kingdom by looking back to such key liberations as God's rescue of the Hebrew people from Egypt, the establishment of a kingdom under David, and God's restoration of the people to Jerusalem after the Babylonian captivity.

Hopes of this kind were not uniquely Jewish, of course. Elsewhere in the Orient, Persian sages looked for the collapse of the Roman empire. To the north the Druids looked for divine aid against Rome, and to the west many looked for the liberation of Spain. The medieval and Renaissance mystique of the eternal Roman empire keeps us from seeing it as both new and potentially unsteady during the first century, although Ramsay MacMullen rightly drew attention to the "enemies of the Roman order" who flourished then.

Royal Messianism and the "Son of David"
at Jerusalem

As with the other groups, the Hebrews had hopes that were both political and religious. Their prophets and psalmists often spoke of the restoration or return of David's ancient kingdom. Prophetic passages[1] include notably Zechariah 12:1–13:1, predicting a victory of the tents of Judah, with the house of David "like God" (12:8). God would provide this kingdom, for when "the children of Israel shall return and seek the Lord their God and David their king" (Hos. 3:5), and "serve the Lord their God and David their king" (Jer. 30:9), God "will set up over them one shepherd, my servant David" (Ezek. 34:23); God's "servant David shall be king over them, and they shall all have one shepherd" (37:24). There were famous Davidic-messianic psalms, notably 2, 72, and 110.

The theme comes back in early Christian tradition, strikingly in relation to Jesus' so-called triumphal entry into Jerusalem. Matthew and Mark tell of crowds shouting, "Blessed is the coming kingdom of our father David" (Mark 11:10, NASV; cf. 10:47) or "Hosanna to the Son of David" (Matt. 21:9). Luke refers to the event as the "visitation" of Jerusalem (19:44) and represents disciples as saying of Jesus, "We had hoped that he was the one to redeem Israel" (24:21). Later they ask him, "Lord, will you at this time restore the kingdom to Israel?" (Acts 1:6) The theme recurs in an early Christian sermon: "Of this man's [David's] posterity God has brought to Israel a Savior, Jesus, as he promised" (Acts 13:23), while according to Romans 1:3 Jesus was "descended from David according to the flesh."[2]

In addition, the genealogies in both Matthew and Luke involve Davidic descent. Matthew 1:1–17 traces the line from Abraham to Joseph through David (largely based on 1 Chronicles 2–3), while Luke 3:23–38 traces it from Joseph back to Adam, also through David. According to the Christian chronicler Julius Africanus, Herod the Great burned such records in "the archives" because of his own low birth, but a few watchful families preserved names from memory or copies.

(Matthew 2:5,16 shows that Herod could be accused of killing David's descendants.) The relatives of Jesus who came from the Galilean villages of Nazareth and Kochaba used such materials for tracing the period after the book of Chronicles.[3]

There was a good deal of controversy over the identity of the—or a—Davidic Messiah. Thus the Jerusalem Christian Hegesippus describes Jewish sects as hostile toward the tribe of Judah and its (Davidic) Messiah and also toward members of the (Davidic) family of Jesus. He believes that the Roman emperors Vespasian, Domitian, and Trajan sought out members of this family in order to prevent insurrection. If he is reliable, he shows that Jerusalem Christians insisted on Jesus' descent from David, and that Jews, Christians, and the Roman authorities thought the question was important. To be sure, opinion was not uniform. *Barnabas* criticizes opponents who "are going to say that the Christ is the son of David" and calls this "the error of the sinners" (12.10). The sinners are evidently Jews, or Jewish Christians with a Christology lower than his own.[4]

The Synoptic Gospels let others call Jesus *christos,* while he himself avoids or sometimes refuses the title. His disciples used the title both before and after his resurrection, though in an early sermon in Acts Peter declares, "Let all the house of Israel therefore know assuredly that God has made him both Lord and Christ, this Jesus whom you crucified" (Acts 2:36). Earlier Peter had said to Jesus, "You are the Christ of God," but "he charged and commanded them to tell this to no one" (Luke 9:20–21 and parallels). Before the high priest he seems to reject the title Christ for himself (Matt. 26:64 and Luke 22:67–68), even though Mark 14:62 represents Jesus as both saying that he *is* the *christos* and predicting the coming of the Son of Man.[5] Mark also expresses the mystery of his being the Christ in his theory of the "messianic secret."

The ordinary Jewish and Jewish Christian interpretation was that the Christ or anointed one would be or was "a man of human descent."[6] Indeed, there is no suggestion in Old Testament texts that an anointed one would be anything but human, and many Gospel texts point in the same direction.

Latent Christology in the Synoptic Gospels

What we may call "latent Christology," a doctrine based on the humanity of Jesus, is often expressed in questions and answers provided by the synoptic evangelists. One good example is in Mark, where a crowd asks after a miracle: "What is this? A new teaching!" (1:27) or again, "Where did this man get all this? What is the wisdom given to him? What mighty works are wrought by his hands!" and they ask the significant question, "Is not this the carpenter, the son of Mary and brother of James and Joses and Judas and Simon, and are not his sisters here with us?" (6:2–3)—though after this question "he could do no mighty work there, except that he laid his hands upon a few sick people and healed them" (6:5). Or again, "We never saw anything like this!" (2:12) Unclean spirits cry out, "You are the Son of God" (3:11), just as the Roman centurion declares, "Truly this man was the Son of God" (15:39). After he stills a storm, his disciples ask, "Who then is this, that even wind and sea obey him?" (4:41) Perhaps the most affirmative summary is this: "He has done all things well" (7:37). In addition, Mark is fond of insisting that individuals and crowds "marveled" or "feared" or "were amazed" or "astounded" at what Jesus said or did (fourteen instances). The other synoptic evangelists make the same point but less frequently.

The comments point to the meaningfulness of the revelation in Jesus, usually in relation to his power, but reasonably enough do not explain rationally or "theologically" who he was. Did the evangelists know? It seems unlikely that there was any one identification. There were partial meanings but ambiguity remained.

Some descriptions offered fairly severe difficulties: for example, Jesus' answer to a man who addressed him as "good teacher": "Why do you call me good? No one is good but God alone" (Mark 10:17–18 and parallels). For another, the saying that "the Son of man came eating and drinking and they say, 'Behold, a glutton and a drunkard, a friend of tax collectors and sinners' " (Matt. 11:18 = Luke 7:34).[7] Such sayings may emerge out of a variety of theological outlooks, or perhaps they expressed what Jesus said on occasions whose contexts were not handed down.

Luke's Special Christology

A view of Jesus as essentially human, though obviously unique, is expressed in the Gospel of Luke, which contains no doctrine of atonement but, instead, a fairly simple teaching about redemption by works. Luke had read in Mark 10:45 that the Son of Man would give his life as "a ransom for many," but he left the expression out as he revised the saying to emphasize Jesus' work as servant.

Luke is the evangelist who describes the infancy of Jesus in relation to development, growth, and obedience and, as we noted, tells in Acts how the earliest preachers pointed to some further change or development, notably after the resurrection. We shall later see Theophilus, a prominent Jewish Christian apologist, making the most of such texts (chapter 5).

The Birth of Jesus

According to Luke the angel Gabriel appeared at Nazareth to Mary, betrothed to Joseph, a descendant of David, and announced that she would conceive and bear a son to be named Jesus; as anointed king he would be called the Son of the Most High and would receive "the throne of his father David" (Luke 1:32). In addition,

> The Holy Spirit will come upon you,
> and the power of the Most High will overshadow you;
> therefore the child to be born will be called holy,
> the Son of God.
>
> Luke 1:35

In the Bible the term "power of the Most High" occurs only in Gabriel's address to Mary. The "atmosphere" of the angel's promise resembles the old stories about the births of Samson and Samuel. His words resemble the predictions of the angel who predicted the birth of Samson to his mother (Judg. 13:2–25) and of the priest Eli that God would give the barren Hannah a son, the future prophet Samuel (1 Sam. 1:17–20). In addition, Luke used Hannah's exultant song as his model for Mary's Magnificat (1 Sam. 2:1–10; Luke 1:46–55).

The Infancy of Jesus

Three "summaries" in Luke's infancy narrative are especially meaningful for his picture of Jesus. He describes the early development of John the Baptist and Jesus, and again uses stereotypes from the biblical account of Samuel. "The child Samuel grew in the presence of the Lord" (1 Sam. 2:21); "the boy Samuel continued to grow both in stature and in favor with the Lord and with men" (2:26); "and Samuel grew, and the Lord was with him" (3:19). So too for Luke "the child [John the Baptist] grew and became strong in spirit" (1:80); "the child [Jesus] grew, and waxed strong in spirit" (2:40, KJV)—or "in wisdom" or "filled with wisdom" (RSV); and "Jesus increased in wisdom and in stature, and in favor with God and man" (2:52). Jesus is essentially a prophet whose infancy foreshadowed his career.

Later on, as pictures of Jesus' human nature came to be more metaphysical and he was viewed as essentially changeless, Luke's language required intensive exegesis, and Jesus' wisdom rather than his growth was emphasized. Justin says that even if Jesus was only human, he was worthy to be called Son of God because of his wisdom.[8] We shall see that Theophilus used this language for his description of Adam in Eden (chapter 5). Origen, however, took it simply and naturally in reference to Jesus and the development of his human soul.[9]

Jesus as Prophet

Naturally Luke emphasizes Jesus' relation to the Holy Spirit, saying that he was "full of the Holy Spirit" and was "led by the Spirit for forty days in the wilderness" (4:1–2).

Later he "returned in the power of the Spirit into Galilee" (4:14) and preached in Nazareth on the text, "The Spirit of the Lord is upon me" (4:18). We recall that "the Spirit of the Lord came mightily" upon Samson (Judg. 14:6), though for more questionable ventures than preaching.[10]

People call Jesus a prophet (Luke 7:16), and he himself calls John the Baptist "more than a prophet" (7:26). The tetrarch Herod is told that in Jesus Elijah has returned, or perhaps "one of the old prophets" (9:8).[11] Thus Jesus is compared with the Old Testament prophets and sometimes with others too, such as Adam, Moses, Joshua, David, and Solomon. Matthew and Luke insist that he was greater than either the wise Solomon or the persuasive Jonah—or even the temple![12] According to Matthew 12:6 he was greater than the temple; Matthew 21:11–12 presents him as "the prophet Jesus from Nazareth of Galilee," visiting Jerusalem to cleanse the temple. Luke tells how after his death some disciples called him "a prophet mighty in deed and word before God and all the people" (24:19).[13] John speaks of him as a unique prophet: "the prophet who is to come into the world" (6:14) or "truly the prophet" (7:40). This is the one whom Moses foretold as like himself and from among his brothers (John 5:46, cf. Deut. 18:15).

Transformations of the Christ

As Christian missionaries went farther out into the Roman world, they paid more attention to that world and its potential for good or ill. They almost always emphasized the first coming of Christ more than a second one. The major letters of Paul reflect two crucial moves made by him or by others. First, he treats the title Messiah or *Christos* as a proper name, not a title, and thus diminishes its special Jewish significance. Second, he finds Christ anticipated in the creation story of Genesis and even in the divine Wisdom of Proverbs. In his early letter to the Corinthians he portrays the Christ both as the Second Adam, like the first human being but superior, and as the Wisdom of God, agent of God in the creation. These passages, not altogether consistent, show that Paul's Christology was rapidly developing and that he was quite willing to speak of Jesus Christ as both human and divine. (For convenience' sake we shall postpone the discussion of Jesus as the Wisdom of God to our next chapter.)

Christological Concepts

It is not surprising that the Gospels contain syntheses of Christological concepts originally independent or even contradictory. Their fusions recall how the Old Testament pictures of God gradually emerged when separate names such as El, Elohim, Elyon, and Yahweh were combined. (The most obvious example is "Yahweh Elohim" in Genesis.) Thus the Gospel of Mark begins and ends with Jesus as Christ and "Son of God" (Mark 1:1, 15:39). According to Acts 2:36 Jesus became "both Lord and Christ." John resembles Mark when he insists "that Jesus is the Christ, the Son of God" (20:31).

Ideas about such concepts as reflecting development or opposition or a mixture of the two probably depend upon trends in exegetical method at various times. Today it is relatively fashionable to insist upon diversity and even conflict within early Christian thought; fifty years ago this was not so common. It is hard to believe that the diversity and conflict have suddenly been discovered and have nothing to do with—for example—the zeal of doctoral dissertation writers for novelty, packaged as discovery. Even a tried-and-true apocalyptic notion like "Son of Man" must be viewed with some caution.

Son of Man

Toward the end of the last century, newly discovered Jewish apocalypses seemed to provide a new background for early Christian thought. At that point the mysterious term *Son of Man* became important for New Testament scholars. They had already seen its importance in the Synoptic Gospels, where Jesus himself is the only one to use it. Now they identified his source in the book of the Secrets of Enoch (1 Enoch

37-71) and, behind that, in the book of Daniel.[14] In Daniel, however, the term means "man" and refers to a human figure coming to God on the clouds of heaven in order to receive an everlasting kingdom (7:13-14); this kingdom is also described as given to "the people of the saints of the Most High" (7:27). And as for Enoch, supposedly the key to Daniel, the section in which "Son of Man" occurs is absent from several Qumran copies, and the term may simply be Christian; John 12:34 represents a Jewish crowd as asking, "Who is this Son of man?"

Apart from the evangelists, early Christians usually neglected the term or took it very simply to mean "man," as in the book of Ezekiel, where God addresses the prophet as "son of man"—a human being. This, after all, is what it means in the Old Testament and in much of the New. Psalm 8 gives a good example: "What is man that you are mindful of him, and the son of man that you care for him?" The parallel shows that "son of man" means "human being." While the epistle to the Hebrews (2:9) refers the psalm to Jesus, perhaps because of "son of man," the usual early patristic interpretation was that Son of Man referred to "Christ as man or Christ's humanity."[15] The term could be correlated with "Son of God," as it was by Ignatius of Antioch: "Jesus Christ, who after the flesh was of the family of David [Rom. 1:3], Son of Man and Son of God."[16] On the other hand, *Barnabas,* probably Alexandrian, insists that Jesus was not son of man but Son of God (12.10).

Justin suggests that Daniel used *"like* a son of man" to hint that while Jesus appeared to be human, and was human, he was not of human origin,[17] while Irenaeus' claim that "the Lord called himself Son of Man to indicate that he was recapitulating the first man in himself"[18] is farfetched and moves toward his own Christological idea that "the Son of God became Son of Man so that . . . man might become a son of God."[19]

Gnostic authors found Son of Man difficult but mysterious enough to incorporate into their systems of primal beings, and some spoke of "Man" or "the First Man" (the god of all);

his Notion, the "son of Man" or "Second Man"; and the Holy Spirit or "Female," who was "borne over the elements: water, darkness, abyss, and chaos" (cf. Gen. 1:3). Both Man and the Son of Man loved the beauty of Spirit, also known as "Mother of the living" (= Eve, Gen. 3:20), and generated the imperishable Logos or Christ. The power of the Female is also known as Wisdom or Male-Female. This picture, which Irenaeus ascribed to the Ophites,[20] shows that Gnostics simply speculated more vigorously than did their more orthodox opponents.

Some Gnostics more reasonably observed that when Jesus uses the expression programmatically—"the Son of Man must be rejected and insulted and crucified"—he "seems to be speaking of someone else, that is, of one who experiences suffering."[21] This interpretation, though based on a docetic Christology, points toward the more modern view that Jesus himself did not make such a prediction, while the evangelist Mark created it from his knowledge of the gospel story.

Bultmann set forth this modern analysis in classical form. There are three kinds of "Son of Man" sayings in the Gospels: (1) apocalyptic, referring to the future coming of the (or a) Son of Man, especially with reference to Daniel 7:13; (2) programmatic and created in the tradition or by the evangelists to summarize Jesus' sufferings, death, and resurrection; and (3) allusive, referring to his present work, to himself, or to humanity in general. The term remains enigmatic. Because of its difficulty (and its use by Gnostics), it was not important for Christology in the early church.

Another Adam

One more Christological term clearly refers to a Jesus who was human though unique. In the epistles of Paul, especially Corinthians and Romans, we encounter a Christ who is beginning a new creation because he is the "second Adam," one who reverses the wrong choice of our common ancestor and, by obeying God instead of disobeying, gives humanity a fresh start.

In 1 Corinthians 15:45–49 Paul correlates the first Adam, the man of earth who "became a living being" (Gen. 2:7), with the last Adam, who came from heaven but "became a life-giving spirit." In Romans 5:12–21 he contrasts the work of the two Adams. The disobedience of the first resulted in condemnation and death, while the obedience of the second resulted in grace, righteousness, acquittal, and life. This picture clearly led up to Irenaeus' theory of "recapitulation" (chapter 7), less obviously to Theophilus' discussion of the first Adam in the light of the second.

The Apostolic Preaching

Such notions as "Son of Man" and "another Adam" do not belong to the common "apostolic preaching" or *kerygma* on which C. H. Dodd and later biblical theologians laid so much emphasis, but we need to recall the preaching in order to suggest that it constituted a major part of the common faith of Christians. Dodd pointed out that in it Jesus was essentially a unique human being. "Jesus of Nazareth, of the lineage of David, had come as Son of God and Messiah." He worked miracles and delivered a new teaching. He was crucified but raised on the third day and exalted to God's right hand. He will come again as judge of the world.[22] This is the *kerygma* which, reiterated by some of the apostolic fathers and Justin, pointed ahead to the old Roman symbol of faith and thence to the Apostles' Creed.

Toward the Divinity of Christ

We conclude that neither "Son of Man" nor "another Adam" modifies the essential humanity of the Jesus set forth in the apostolic preaching. In order for his divinity to be recognized, we must follow the apostolic teaching about his relation to the Father as Creator, and to that we now turn.

2
Biblical Christology: The Divinity of Christ

Some modern scholars have suggested that Jesus never lived or was an Essene or a magician, while Christianity arose out of mystery religions or Gnostic ideas. There has been widespread enthusiasm for "divine men" in the Greco-Roman world, including Palestine, with such figures supposedly influencing portrayals of Jesus as early as the time of 2 Corinthians.[1] The "typical divine man" had been reconstructed by Ludwig Bieler in his *Theios Aner* of 1935–36, but the book came into its own chiefly in the 1960s as scholars found in it one more way of rewriting the story of Jesus. Here we are not concerned with the controversies over the existence, categorization, influence, or relevance of these men but simply with a few semifactual cases permitting some relation to Christology.

The most useful examples come from Judaea not long after the time of Jesus.[2] They are important because the author of the book of Acts himself saw that outsiders could regard them as parallels (Acts 5:36–37; 21:38). In his *War* Josephus described "deceivers and impostors" who claimed "divine possession" (*theiasmos*) and led many to the desert for "signs of liberation." The Roman authorities responded with cavalry and infantry (2.259). Again, an "Egyptian false prophet" led a throng from the desert to the Mount of Olives, promising to enter the city of Jerusalem and become "tyrant," presumably king. He too was defeated before he could attack (2.261–263). Josephus later rewrote the narratives in his *Antiquities*

(20.167–72). This time he laid emphasis on the "evident wonders and signs in harmony with God's providence" that were to be effected in the desert, as well as on the miracle promised by the Egyptian, who wanted to stand on the Mount of Olives and make the city walls of Jerusalem fall down. Evidently he planned to recapitulate the miracle of Joshua, who flattened the walls of Jericho by divine guidance (Joshua 6). Josephus also told of a pseudoprophet who persuaded many to follow him to the Jordan, which would be parted at his command (20.97–98). Again the story of Joshua is in view (Joshua 3–4). In other words, while these miracles, or those of Jesus, can be viewed as like those of Hellenistic "divine men," their basic setting lies in Old Testament stories taken as "types" of later events.[3]

By themselves such miracles would not prove the divinity of the miracle worker. Opponents of Christianity did not usually try to disprove the miracles of Jesus but ascribed them to magic without questioning the events themselves. On the other hand, Origen certainly coordinated "divine nature" with "miracles" (e.g., *Against Celsus* 3.29), and a very late fragment ascribed to Melito of Sardis claims that Jesus proved his humanity in the thirty years before his baptism, when he "hid the signs of his deity," and then proved his deity "through the signs in the three years after the baptism."[4] Belief in the divinity of Christ did not originally rest on such foundations, however.

Christ as the Image of God

We have already mentioned Paul's picture of Christ as the Second Adam, which obviously drew attention to the creation story and thus pointed beyond Adam toward Christ as the Image of God, the Wisdom of God, and—ultimately—God; that is to say, toward the divine titles that were to give patristic Christology its basic impetus.

Since Adam was originally created after God's image and likeness (Gen. 1:26–27), whatever is said of the Second Adam must be related to this image. Christ restored the image lost

in the Fall, and whoever looks at Christ sees humanity as it
was meant to be. Satan blinded unbelievers to keep them
from seeing "the light of the gospel of the glory of Christ, who
is the image of God" (2 Cor. 4:4, NASV), but God "has shone in
our hearts to give the light of the knowledge of the glory of
God in the face of Christ" (4:6). Here the language may echo
the Wisdom of Solomon 7:25, which speaks of Wisdom as
"the pure emanation of the glory of the Almighty." Its theological base may also go back to Philo, who further developed
a doctrine of image by claiming that God first produced the
divine Image, the Logos, and then made humanity in accordance with it.[5] Though Paul touches on the theme only in 2
Corinthians 4, it is congruent with other Pauline ideas, especially those concerning God's Wisdom. To be sure, Paul also
discusses man as the image and glory of God and woman as
merely the glory of her husband (1 Cor. 11:7), but this idea
seems an aberration when compared with the Christological
thrust of his teaching generally.[6]

Obedience, Adam, and image underline the magnificent
hymn in Philippians, where Paul sings of the complete obedience, not disobedience, of the one in God's image and of his
exaltation when he is given "the name above every name."

> Though being in the form of God
> he did not consider equality with God a prize
> but emptied himself,
> assuming the form of a slave
> and coming to be in the likeness of men;
> he humbled himself,
> becoming obedient unto death,
> death on a cross.
> Therefore God highly exalted him
> and gave him the name, the name above every name,
> so that in the name of Jesus
> every knee might bend,
> of beings heavenly and earthly and subterranean,
> and every tongue confess that
> Jesus Christ is Lord
> to the glory of God the Father.·
>
> Philippians 2:6–11

Admittedly exegesis is difficult. He was in the form of God, as Adam was in the image of God. Why would he have grasped at equality with God—to retain it or to gain it? If we take our clue from the story of the first Adam, we find the serpent telling Eve that if she and Adam eat from the tree of knowledge they will "be like gods, knowing good and evil" (Gen. 3:5). God later says that Adam "has become like one of us" (3:22). Perhaps Jesus in his obedience reversed Adam's fall, though he was not just another Adam, since he came to be "in the likeness of men." The hymn now turns to the earthly obedience of Jesus that led to the cross and, through the cross, to his exaltation and recognition as "Lord," a Greek term equivalent to the Hebrew *Adonai* and also used of God in the Bible. Paul's model may be not Adam but something more than Adam, the Image of God after whose likeness Adam was made.

Philippians tells of the work of Christ Jesus, who was "in the form of God" but "divested himself, taking the form of a slave." Because of his subsequent obedience God exalted him and gave him "the name above every name." Jesus was redoing and undoing the disobedience of Adam, perhaps step by step. (Patristic interpretations, equally speculative, are discussed by F. Loofs[7] and J. Gewiess.[8])

But what was the Image after which Adam was created? In Genesis 1:26–27 it is not explained; the expression simply means that Adam, humanity, was like God. Speculative exegetes looked for more detail, however, and when they found in the book of Proverbs God's Wisdom explaining how she took part in the work of creation, they proceeded to identify Image as Wisdom. According to the Wisdom of Solomon (7:26) Wisdom is "a reflection of eternal light, spotless mirror of the working of God, and an image of his goodness." The way was being opened to treat divine attributes as persons.

(In addition to image, the creation story uses *likeness,* a term which Philo sensibly says was added just for the sake of exactness.[9] New Testament writers do not differentiate image from likeness. Such subtlety was reserved for the Gnostics and Irenaeus.)

Sophia or Wisdom of God

Paul or an anonymous predecessor took another step when he or she identified Jesus Christ with the heavenly Wisdom of Proverbs. The notion is not synoptic, for three "wisdom" texts in Matthew and Luke do not make the identification. Luke 11:49 records as a saying of Jesus, "Therefore also the Wisdom of God said, 'I will send them prophets and apostles,'" but Jesus is not Wisdom. Luke 7:35 (= Matt. 11:19) says that "Wisdom is justified," but it is not clear how. The most important text, Matthew 11:28–30, presents Jesus as speaking in the name of the Wisdom of God, just as Ben Sira does at the end of his book (51:23, 26–27), referring to the Wisdom that had come forth from God's mouth (24:3).

Matthew 11:28–30	Sirach 51:23, 26–27
Come to me,	Draw near to me,
all you who labor	you who are untaught
under burdens	
and I will give you rest.	and lodge in my school.
Take my yoke upon you	Put your neck under the yoke,
and learn from me,	and
for I am lowly and humble	let your
of heart,	souls
and you will find rest	receive
for your souls;	instruction;
for my yoke is easy	it is to be found close by.
and my burden is light.	See that I have labored little
	and received much rest.

The text is important because it hints that the divine Wisdom was speaking through Jesus or that he was speaking in her name; but it does not give him a superhuman status, any more than the verses in Sirach make their author into the Wisdom of God.

The principal Old Testament text used in support of the doctrine was Proverbs 8:22–25, where Wisdom says (in Greek),

> The Lord created me as the beginning for his works,
> before the ages he established me in the beginning.

> Before he made the earth and the abysses . . .
> before all the hills he generated me.

While the term "created" clearly appears in verse 22, it is replaced by "generated" in verse 25, making the text even more appropriate for Christology. Later verses simply emphasize the presence of Wisdom at the creation. Thus verse 27 says that "when he established the heavens, I was there," and verses 29–30 make the same point: "When he made strong the foundations of the earth I was with him, setting them in order." A briefer version occurs in Proverbs 3:19–20:

> God by Wisdom established the earth,
> he prepared the heavens by Understanding;
> by Perception the abysses broke forth,
> and the clouds drop down dew.

Both texts appear among second-century Christian theologians.

Scholars have sometimes claimed that the model for Wisdom was the Egyptian goddess Isis, but it appears that the cosmic mediatrix Isis depicted in Greek hymns is later than Proverbs itself. The picture of Isis as active in the creation was not the source used by Proverbs but provided a milieu in which Jewish and Christian claims could be intelligible.[10]

Wisdom was thus the divine being through whom God made the world and everything in it; and she is the person, or personification, with whom Paul identifies Christ. We have already alluded to the key passage, virtually creedal, in which Paul contrasts idolatrous polytheism with Christian faith (1 Cor. 8:6).

> For us there is
> one God, the Father,
> for whom is everything and
> for whom we exist; and
> one Lord, Jesus Christ,
> through whom is everything and
> through whom we exist.

Clearly Christ's function in creation is that of the heavenly

Wisdom whose portrait in Proverbs was developed in Hellenistic Judaism. The name occurs in 1 Corinthians, not only in
1:30, where Christ Jesus is described as having become Wisdom from God for us (as well as righteousness, holiness, and
redemption), but precisely in 1:24: "Christ the power of God
and the wisdom of God." The prepositions ring the changes
on the principal Hellenistic idea of causation, set forth for example by Philo: "by whom" as the first cause, "from what" the
material, "through what" the instrument, "for what" the end
or object. He identifies the first cause as God, the material as
the four elements, the instrument as the Logos, and the final
cause as the goodness of the Demiurge or Fashioner.[11]

In Colossians 1:15–18 the key word is *image* but the description is based on Wisdom as interpreted by rabbinic
rules. Christ

> is the Image of the invisible God,
> firstborn of the whole creation.
> For *in* him all things were created
>   in the heavens and on the earth,
>   visible and invisible,
>   Thrones, Lordships, Principalities, Powers;
> all were created *through* him and *for* him;
> and he is *before* all
> and all hold *together in* him.

Similar language is then applied to salvation through Christ.
The point is that if one could say that *in* Wisdom creation
took place one could also speak of creation *through* and *for*
and *before*. The prepositions are more or less interchangeable,
just as they are in 1 Corinthians 8:6.[12]

Sophia or Logos?

It should be added that the gender question arose very
early. *Sophia* is obviously feminine. How then is it related to
the Son of God? Philo gave a vigorously sexist explanation:
Her name is feminine, but her nature is masculine. She is
subordinate to the male Father as "the female always comes
short of the male and is less than it."[13] Origen drops the ex-

planation but says "we should not imagine that because of the feminine name wisdom and righteousness are feminine in their being."[14] The existence of the problem may help explain why the masculine word *Logos* came to be preferred. In addition it had links with philosophy.

So then we come to the picture of Christ as the Word or Logos of God in the prologue to the Gospel of John. The language is basically derived from Old Testament statements about Wisdom, correlated with the creative Word that God spoke at the beginning of creation: "Let there be Light." We may compare Psalm 33:6:

> By the Word of the Lord the heavens were founded
> and by the breath [*pneuma*] of his mouth all their strength.

The "word" is evidently the creative word of Genesis and God's "breath" is the *pneuma* above the waters. Hellenistic Jews closely associated Wisdom and Word and sometimes considered them identical.[15] John uses prepositions in the Pauline and Philonic manner when he describes creation. The first section concerns the relation of the Logos to God, as Bultmann pointed out.

> In the beginning was the Logos
> and the Logos was *with* God
> and the Logos was God.
> It was with God in the beginning.
> Everything came to be *through* it,
> And *nothing* came to be *apart from* it.
> What came to be *in* it was life,
> and the life was the light of humanity.
>
> John 1:1–4

Most of these terms, as Bultmann indicated after J. Rendel Harris,[16] have some connection with the Wisdom literature of the Old Testament and the apocrypha. He did not believe, however, that "Jewish speculation" was the source of the prologue. Instead, he had already claimed that much of the Wisdom literature was strongly influenced by Gnostic mythology. The prologue, therefore, was Gnostic in origin, as is the idea of the incarnation of the Savior.[17] This seems mistaken. A much simpler explanation can be based on the text of Genesis. The Logos is what God *said,* and what God said was, "Let there be light." This light preceded the creation of living beings and could be regarded as identical with life.

Later theologians insisted that, like Sophia, the Logos was originally *in* God. Gnostics[18] agreed with Theophilus, Irenaeus, and Clement that the evangelist John meant "in God" when he said that "the Logos was *pros ton theon,*"[19] though Justin and Irenaeus also said the Logos was "with God."[20] Tertullian[21] finally renounced the idea, but followers of Paul of Samosata[22] picked it up again, as did Marcellus of Ancyra. Presumably it won favor for a time because of the Johannine emphasis on the coinherence of the Father with the Son. Marcellus argued that the Logos was in the Father because of John 1:1 ("in the Beginning") and John 10:38 ("the Father is in me and I am in the Father").[23]

Theologians interpreted the work of the Logos in different ways. Some certainly spoke of incarnation, while Theophilus never mentioned it, as we shall see.

The second section of the prologue deals with the relation of the Logos to the world.

> The light shines in the darkness,
> and the darkness did not grasp [*katelaben*] it. . . .
> It was the true light,
> which illuminates every one,
> that was coming into the world.
> [It was in the world,
> and] the world came to be through it,
> and the world did not know it.
> It came to its own,
> but its own did not accept [*parelabon*] it.
> But whoever did receive it, it gave them
> the power to become children of God—
> those who believe in its name
> and were born not of the will of the flesh,
> nor of the will of human beings,
> but of God.
>
> John 1:5–13

Here again we find echoes of Genesis, where there is a primal darkness above the abyss, and God separates the light from the darkness. A rather dualistic phrase in 2 Corinthians (6:14) illustrates the contrast: "What fellowship [does] light have with darkness?" Apparently the subject is shifting from creation to redemption but without any explanation of the way in which the Logos "came to its own."

Finally we reach the unique incarnation and self-revelation of the Logos.

> And the Logos became flesh
> and tabernacled among us,
> and we beheld its glory,
> glory as of the only Son of the Father,
> full of grace and truth. . . .
> Of its abundance we have all received,
> and grace upon grace;
> for the law was given through Moses,
> but grace and truth came to be through Jesus Christ.
> No one has ever seen God;
> God the only Son, in the bosom of the Father,
> has made him known.
>
> John 1:14–18

This section of the poem or hymn speaks of the incarnation or "infleshment" of the Logos and the consequent self-revelation of the Son Jesus Christ. Bultmann rightly insisted in his commentary that "the Logos became flesh" had no Jewish antecedents. Even though Celsus supposes that Jews could speak of the Logos (as Philo did) and call it Son of God, they could not accept incarnation.[24] Bultmann's further claim, however, that "the evangelist adopted the mythological language of Gnosis"[25] seems wrong. The early Gnostics spoke of the Savior not as incarnate but as disguised in flesh and human only in semblance (see chapter 3). The Valentinian Ptolemaeus explained John 1:14 away as simply telling the names of aeons in the Pleroma: Father, Grace, Only-begotten, and Truth.[26] A variant of this view seems to appear in the recent and thorough study by Michael Theobald.[27] He argues that incarnation Christology is an answer to a semi-Gnostic Wisdom Christology, not a development out of it.

However it may have originated, non-Gnostic writers followed John and insisted on the literal incarnation of which he spoke. *2 Clement* 9.5 says of Christ that "though he was originally spirit, he became flesh and so called us." Doubtless he should have said that the Logos became incarnate, not Christ. But when he adds, "Let us love one another, so that we may come into the kingdom of God" (9.6), we see him continuing to reflect Johannine ideas.[28] Justin echoes John in similar fashion when he writes of the way "our Savior Jesus Christ was made flesh through the Logos and bore flesh and blood for our salvation,"[29] thus joining *2 Clement* by identifying Christ with Logos.

Son of God

For Philo, the Logos is the "firstborn Son" of God, while in "Hellenistic mysticism" it could be said that "the luminous Logos derived from Mind is the Son of God."[30] Christian use of the term develops from Son to Logos, not from Logos to Son. Parallels with Philo therefore show what the term came to mean, not how it began.

Mark's Gospel probably started thus: "Beginning of the gospel of Jesus Christ, the Son of God." Why Son of God? According to Luke 3:22 a heavenly voice at his baptism declared, "Thou art my beloved Son, with thee I am well pleased" or, in the Western text and early fathers, "You are my Son, today I have begotten you" (Ps. 2:7). This theological story might be the source of the idea, but it is not at all certain that the exegesis of the psalm came before the use of the title. The early genealogy of Luke 3:23–38 ends with "Adam, the son of God," though the genealogy of Matthew 1:16 ends with Jesus "who is called Christ."

Matthew 24:36 follows Mark 13:32 in stating that "no one knows, not even the angels . . . nor the Son, but the Father only" about the end time. Here, as in another text about the mutual knowledge of the Father and the Son (Matt. 11:25–27 paradox, and to him we owe the Christological paradox of 1 Corinthians 1:23–25.

> We preach Christ crucified,
> a scandal to the Jews and
> foolishness to the gentiles:
> but to those who are called,
> whether Jews or Greeks,
> Christ the Power of God and
> the Wisdom of God.

Elsewhere Paul speaks less paradoxically and refers to the one Christ who "loved me and gave himself for me" (Gal. 2:20). Or again, "though he was rich, yet for your sake he became poor, so that by his poverty you might become rich" (2 Cor. 8:9).

In addition, Paul's statements about his own experience show how he could hold suffering and power together. He insists that he is strong when he is weak but then turns to "boast," claiming that his "signs and wonders and miracles" prove he is an apostle (2 Cor. 12:10, 12). Weakness and strength are not diametrically opposed. Indeed, Christ said to him, "My grace is sufficient for you, for my power is made perfect in weakness" (12:9).

The Preaching of Peter and Ignatius of Antioch

A philosophical theology derived from Middle Platonism first clearly appears in the apocryphal *Preaching of Peter*. God is "the unseen who sees all, the uncontained who contains all, the one beyond need whom all things need, . . . uncreated who created all by the word of his power (that is, the Son)."[33] When the Son himself was called God, these epithets had to be reexamined if his humanity was not to be undermined.

Ignatius of Antioch reflects such reconsideration. He speaks of Christ as "above seasons, timeless, unseen who for us became seen; who cannot be touched,[34] who cannot suffer but for us accepted suffering, who in every way endured for us."[35] Evidently both Ignatius and his opponents used the divine epithets of both God and Christ. Unlike them he used paradox based on redemption ("for us") in speaking of Christ's human nature and thus followed the example of Paul. Not every theologian would feel free to do so.

3
Gnostic Christologies

In spite of the exciting and valuable Gnostic documents re-
covered from Nag Hammadi in Egypt, the basic starting point
for the study of the Gnostics has to lie in the earliest criti-
cisms by Christians who wrote against heresies. These authors provide the only chronology there is, and their accounts
of the earliest systems are the only ones there are. They are
especially valuable to us because of their emphasis on Christology.

Simon Magus

The early Fathers agree that Simon Magus—perhaps the
magician described in Acts 8, perhaps not—was the first
Gnostic. He cannot be called a *Christian* Gnostic, however,
for his disciples regarded him, not Jesus, as the manifestation
of God. Both he and his disciple Menander were said to have
claimed to be supreme creators and redeemers. There is no
Simonian doctrine of Christ, but there may (or may not) be an
analogous development.

Justin Martyr says that Samaritans and a few others ac-
knowledged Simon as the First God and said that his consort
Helen, a former prostitute, had been the creative First
Thought of his mind.[1]

Simon's Thought

Thirty years later, Irenaeus provided further details about both Helen and Simon. The clearer picture of Helen as a cosmic figure seems to owe much to the Wisdom of God with whom Jesus had already been identified. According to Simon,

> she was the First Thought of his mind, the Mother of All, through whom at the beginning he thought of making angels and archangels. This Thought leapt forth from him; she knew her father's purpose; she descended to the lower regions and generated the angels and powers by whom this world was made.

Similarly in the Wisdom of Solomon Wisdom is the "mother" of all good things (7:12), and God's "all-powerful word leaped from heaven out of the royal throne" at the exodus (18:15). This Wisdom must have descended to earth, for she "cries aloud in the street and raises her voice in the markets" (Prov. 1:20, cf. 8:2).

In addition, the Simonians were influenced by pagan mythology, for they prayed to images of Simon as Zeus and Helen as Athena. This was important because Greek allegorizers had already named Zeus the supreme god; Athena's birth from his head was the expression of his thought (see chapter 5).

Thought in Chains

Thought's primeval struggle with the angels is described in two accounts of the events, apparently different, both reproduced by Irenaeus (see texts below). The first account tells how the angels were envious of Thought's creative capacity; they pretended they had created or generated themselves. The second account treats them as merely perverse, eager to keep her in captivity.

In either case she seems to be very much like the human soul, imprisoned and mistreated in the body. Her story has nothing to do with the story of Jesus and his life among humans. It has emerged from a pessimistic, dualistic worldview basically alien to both Judaism and Christianity. Here are the stories:[2]

1	2
	Simon was quite unknown to them,
but after she generated them she was held captive by them out of envy, since they did not want to be considered the offspring of anyone else.	but his Thought was held captive by the powers and angels she had emitted
	and she suffered complete disgrace from them, unable to return upward to her father.

> She was enclosed in a human body,
> and through the ages passed into other female
>   bodies,
> as from one vase to another.

What concerned the Simonians, or Irenaeus himself, was Helen more than Simon. They claimed that Simon's Thought was in Helen of Troy, and they believed that she had been slandered by the many classical authors who claimed she caused the Trojan war.[3] Edgar Allan Poe reiterates the ancient theme when he speaks of her "face that launched a thousand ships and burnt the topless towers of Ilium." The Simonians also provided a philosophical-theological statement about her decline and total fall.

> She transmigrated from body to body
> and always suffered disgrace;
> last of all she was in a brothel;
> she was the "lost sheep" [Luke 15:6].

Helen is important for us as the inconstant incarnation of a divine being. More important, her fallen situation explains the descent of Simon from heaven. On the Christian view, Christ came to save a fallen world, but the supreme deity of the Simonians came down to rescue his own Thought, imprisoned by the fallen angels she had generated. Like later Gnostics, Simonians probably ascribed to the ignorant demiurge, one of these angels, the words, "You shall have no other gods before me; . . . I . . . am a jealous god" (Exod. 20:3–5). Such a god obviously "desired the primacy."

| | When the angels misgoverned the world, since each one desired the primacy, |
| He himself came in order to recover her and set her free from bonds, and provide salvation by the Gnosis of himself. | he came down in order to correct the situation. |

Simon's Descent

The Simonian myth tells of coming down from heaven but explicitly denies that the Redeemer became incarnate.

> Simon descended, transformed and made like the principalities and powers and angels, so that among men he appeared as a man, though he was not a man, and he was thought to suffer in Judaea, though he did not suffer.

Another statement tries to correlate Simonian doctrine with some kind of Christianity and with gentile religion.

> He appeared among the Jews as Son, came down in Samaria as Father [i.e., as Simon], and came among the other nations as Holy Spirit. He was the Supreme Power, that is, the Father who is above all, and he consented to be called whatever men call him.[4]

Simonianism was thus highly syncretistic and accommodating, borrowing or stealing much from early Christianity. All it rejected was physical reality and practical morality.

Liberation from the Inferior Angels

A further comment deals with inspiration and redemption and uses even more Christian language. "The prophets spoke the prophecies under the inspiration of the angels who made

who made the world, especially
the god of the Jews.[6]

In the first version, but not the second, "the god of the Jews"
is one of the archons or angels hostile to the Father. Christ
came to destroy this god and save believers, just as according
to 1 John 3:8 "the Son of God appeared in order to destroy the
works of the devil." We should expect that for Saturninus the
god of the Jews was the devil, but the discussion of Satan
suggests that he was not. Satan instituted marriage and generation (which are bad) since he was present in Eden in or as
the serpent. Some of the Old Testament prophecies come
from Satan, others from the angels who made the world. Indeed, Satan is the enemy of the angels and especially the god
of the Jews, and Christ and his Father are also opposed to
them. Is not, then, Satan an ally of Christ and the god above?
The account looks confused, but part of it may be lacking.

The other version explains that the angels made both evil
and good races. Presumably Saturninus did not have Cain
and Abel in mind, for they were not made by angels, but relied
on Genesis 1:27: "male and female made he them." Ecclesiastes 7:28, a verse used by other Gnostics, could be a proof text:
"One man [*adam*] among a thousand I found, but a woman
among all these I have not found." Indeed, another point
could come from the very next verse in Ecclesiastes: "This
alone have I found, that [*Elohim*] made man upright." (Elohim would thus be contrasted with either Yahweh or Yahweh
Elohim.)

As for redemption, the Savior, who is not called Christ in
this narrative, came to fight the demons who aided the evil, to
destroy the evil and to save the good. Since he was a spiritual
being, he merely seemed to be human. These accounts do not
contradict each other but express Saturninus' ideas from different angles. The first of them is especially hostile toward
"the god of the Jews," while the other comes from garden-
variety Gnosticism.

Saturninus' reference to "the god of the Jews" and his two
enemies, Christ and Satan, must be related to the historical

events of his time. Irenaeus gives his date when he calls him a contemporary of Basilides, a teacher under Hadrian (117–38) who also spoke of "the god of the Jews." Since Eusebius dates Basilides precisely at the beginning of the Jewish revolt of 132–35,[7] we suspect that the term "the god of the Jews" reflects this event. It produced strong anti-Jewish sentiment among both Romans and Christians, as both Justin and Aristo of Pella indicate.[8] Presumably it also influenced the thought of Saturninus, Basilides, and Marcion.

Basilides of Alexandria

The doctrine of Basilides of Alexandria may have been more important because of its greater sophistication, though this may not have won converts. Of the two accounts of what Basilides taught, the one in Irenaeus probably comes from the heresiarch, while later disciples gave information to Hippolytus.

Primary Psychological Emanations

In Basilides' chain of emanations from the "unbegotten Father," Logos is merely a personified moment in the psychological process of thought and creativity and is subordinate to Mind as well as to the Father. The sequence of emanations is quite unlike the Logos doctrine in the Gospel of John and moves toward greater complexity and psychological theory. It is not clear that this is an improvement, any more than is Basilides' notion that there are 365 heavens.[9]

Earthly Affairs

His Christology emerges when he discusses the lowest heaven, our own. The chief of the angels who made it

> is the one considered the god of the Jews. Since he wanted to subject the other peoples to his own people, the Jews, all the rest of the rulers arose against him and took action against him

[Ps. 2:2]. Therefore the other nations [Ps. 2:1] rose up against his people.[10]

This statement clearly reflects the Jewish revolts of 115–17 and 132–35, which were suppressed by "the other nations" and their rulers, angelic or human. At this point Basilides' chronology is obviously in error, but it was not his major concern.

> But the ungenerated and unnameable Father, seeing their destruction, sent his firstborn Mind, who is called Christ, to free those who believe him from the power of those who made the world, and he appeared to their peoples on earth as a man and performed miracles. <Since he was Mind> he did not suffer, but a certain Simon of Cyrene was impressed to carry his cross for him and because of ignorance and error was crucified, transformed by him so that he might be thought to be Jesus. Jesus himself took on the form of Simon and stood there deriding them [Ps. 2:4]. Since he was the incorporeal Power and Mind of the ungenerated Father, he was transformed as he wished and thus ascended to him who had sent him, deriding them, since he could not be held and was invisible to all.

The Coptic *Gospel of Philip* says that "some have entered the kingdom of heaven laughing," but that is a different idea.

The basic doctrine is much the same as that of Saturninus, but Basilides was acquainted with obscure details in the Gospel of Mark and in Psalm 2, on which his story about Christ is based. Mark gave him the story of Simon of Cyrene and his bearing "his" cross (Mark 15:21). The name of Jesus is not mentioned in this story before Mark 15:34, and even then not in the popular version reflected by Codex Bezae and the Koridethi manuscript. A severe literalist could argue that Simon was crucified. Again, Psalm 2 begins,

> Why do the nations conspire,
>   and the peoples plot in vain?
> The kings of the earth set themselves,
>   and the rulers [*archontes*] take counsel together,
>   against the Lord and his anointed.

But they have gone astray:

> He who sits in the heavens laughs;
>   the Lord has them in derision.
> Then he will speak to them in his wrath,
>   and terrify them in his fury.

Christians generally found meaning in verse 7 of Psalm 2: "You are my son, today I have begotten you," but Basilides found a more esoteric doctrine in the first two verses of the psalm.

Denying Christ Crucified

This kind of exegesis had practical consequences, for if Christ was not crucified there was no special reason to confess his name in times of persecution.

> Those who know these things are freed from the principalities who made the world and one must not confess the one who was crucified but the one who came in the form of a man and was thought to be crucified, and was called Jesus, and was sent by the Father so that by this plan he might destroy the works of those who made the world. If anyone confesses the crucified one he is still a slave and under the power of those who made bodies; he who denies is freed from them, for he knows the plan of the ungenerated Father.

The special Gnostic exegesis results in a special way of life with the rejection of Christianity.

Marcion and His Gospel

Another Gnostic who taught at precisely the same time was Marcion, well known for his *Gospel, Apostle,* and *Antitheses.* He claimed that his *Gospel* was the authentic version of what the churches read as Luke, while his *Apostle* contained the authentic letters of Paul. His basic theory was that *the* gospel, known to Paul, had been "interpolated by the defenders of Judaism," who corrupted it as they also corrupted Paul's letters.

Like other Gnostics he was reacting against the Jewish revolt of 132–35, which had taken place only a few years before he left his native Pontus for Rome (138–39). Presumably the tragic end of the revolt influenced him as he tried to disentangle the Gospel from the Old Testament and insisted that the Old Testament messiah was a warrior who promised the restoration of Israel, while "our Christ" treated the kingdom of God as "an eternal and celestial possession." For Marcion the kingdom of God was Christ himself.[11]

We saw other Gnostics differentiating "the god of the Jews," the creator, from the unknown Father above him, from whom the Christ had come. Marcion's idea was slightly more nuanced. He too held that the creator was ignorant of the good God above him, known only to Jesus, but admitted that he was just and devoted to law. Harnack says that for him the good God was "love, nothing but love," but provides no evidence. Since Marcion taught that Christ appeared and suffered only in appearance, he must have displeased many Christians.[12] Nevertheless, the powerfully dualistic doctrine was able to survive in the Roman church for five or six years until his excommunication in 144.

It is possible that his attack on the Pauline epistles kept Justin from quoting them in his *Apologies* and *Dialogue*. His negative ideas about the Gospels inevitably slowed down development of the doctrine of Christ. How could the churches rely on falsified documents?

Jesus Among the Valentinians

The disciples of Valentinus too were concerned with the Gospels and Christology. They explained the mysterious expressions about Jesus' origin in Luke 1:35 by holding that "Spirit" referred to the aeon Sophia, active in shaping the spiritual body of the Lord, while "Power" from the inferior creator god shaped his physical body.[13] In the same verses of Luke a rather eccentric Valentinian teacher named Mark the Magician found the powers that emanated from the Second Tetrad and generated the Jesus who appeared on earth. These were the angel Gabriel (Luke 1:26), i.e., the Logos; Holy Spirit

(1:35), i.e., Life; Power of the Most High (1:35), i.e., Man; and Virgin (1:27), i.e., Church.[14]

All Valentinians knew that Luke secretly expressed their doctrine in his early canticles[15] and the details about Jesus' early development. Theodotus fancifully suggested that taken together these details explain how Jesus took on the psychic element, which needed to grow in size (Luke 1:80 = 2:40), as well as the spiritual so that he would advance in wisdom or Sophia.[16] He developed further Christological doctrines out of other Gospels and held that Jesus was "different from the elements he assumed." Jesus obviously spoke in his own name when he said, "I am the Life," "I am the Truth," and "I and the Father are one" (John 11:25, 14:6, 10:30). He referred to someone else when he said that the Son of Man must be rejected, insulted, crucified (Mark 8:31, etc.), using the third person for speaking of the merely psychic Christ.[17] In essence, Theodotus is making his point by contrasting the Christ of the Synoptic Gospels with the Jesus of John.[18]

According to Theodotus, Jesus himself was responsible for the differences in the Gospels because he taught the apostles in different ways, first in figures and mysteries, later in parables and enigmas (cf. Mark 4:34), and at the end clearly and openly, when they were alone (John 16:19).[19] The Gnostic teacher has thus made a system out of the tradition and has chosen what was said "clearly and openly" for himself.[20]

We have already touched upon another way of classifying texts in the Gospels, this time by ascribing some of them to early and misguided disciples. The classification originated with Marcion, who thought the early Jewish disciples interpolated the true gospel to make it seem more Jewish than it was; they added the birth stories and emphasized the fulfillment of prophecy.[21]

According to all these systems there was a gradual development in the teaching of Jesus or in the apostolic preaching about him or in both. The idea of development enabled exegetes to discover the more perfect and Gnostic teaching—that is, their own—that lay beneath the surface of the texts.

Carpocrates on Christ

One more sect deserves attention because it laid emphasis on the human Jesus but developed Christology in a Gnostic direction. The Carpocratians held that the pure soul of Jesus, son of Joseph, remembered what it had seen above. The unbegotten Father therefore sent a power to release him from the angels who made the world, and by its aid he learned to despise his ancestral Jewish customs. Carpocrates thus made Jesus like the Paul of Galatians 1:10–14, and some of his followers declared themselves equal to Jesus or above him because of their greater contempt for the angels, especially the god of the Jews and his law. For this esoteric group Jesus was evidently human. They could demonstrate their own contempt for the angels by going beyond good and evil, which exist only in human opinion, "doing everything" and escaping reincarnation. This counsel is what Jesus secretly gave his disciples and apostles. They were to transmit it to those who were worthy (cf. Mark 4:11, 34).[22]

At Alexandria Clement knew of a "secret gospel" of Mark, a gospel which Carpocrates had interpolated with his own "shameless lies." Unfortunately, he does not quote from Carpocrates' version, though he says that an earlier "secret" version of Mark treated Jesus as a "hierophant," founder of "the great mysteries" of the Alexandrian church.[23] Such a view of Jesus is consistent with what Carpocrates tells about him as the teacher of secrets.

4

Christology in the Apostolic Fathers and Justin

We now turn to more "orthodox" developments around the time of the early Gnostics, and first among those later called the "apostolic fathers." Their purely informal title indicates that later Christians considered them relatively close to the apostles in time and in doctrine. They reflect a wide geographical spread. In essence, they are authors later approved by such figures as Irenaeus and Clement of Alexandria, and they include a catechetical manual, the *Didache*, perhaps from Syria, and writings by Clement and Hermas of Rome, Ignatius of Antioch and his colleague Polycarp of Smyrna, and Barnabas, probably from Alexandria. They are sometimes treated as if they expressed a common view of Christian theology, but they can better be viewed as trying to counter the Gnostic Christologies with rather simple doctrines of their own.

The *Didache*

The Didachist's traditional ideas are best set forth in his liturgical prayers, in which he first repeats the Matthaean baptismal formula about baptizing "in the name of the Father and of the Son and of the Holy Spirit" (7.1–2; Matt. 28:19) but does not explain what the terms mean. Next he refers to the prayer "as the Lord commanded in his gospel" (8.2; Matt. 6:5, 9–13). Finally he sets forth eucharistic prayers that refer to Jesus as the child of "our" Father, who revealed the holy vine of David, as well as life, knowledge, faith, and immortality, and gave Christians spiritual food and drink and eternal life (9–10). There seems to be no specific doctrine of divine sonship, and Jesus is essentially a revealer and teacher rather than a mediator—just as the eucharist in the *Didache* (if it is a eucharist) contains no reference to the Last Supper or the words of institution. The *Didache* reflects tradition but does not defend it, explain it, or develop it.

Clement of Rome

Clement of Rome may have written around the same time, making use of traditional Jewish terms such as "the scepter of the greatness of God" (16.2) and also stating that "his blood was poured out for our salvation and brought the grace of repentance to the world" (7.4) and was "given for us" (21.6). God is the sole Creator who made humankind "by his sacred and faultless hands" (33.4)—without reference to Christ. Even though Clement evidently echoes the opening chapters of Hebrews in his whole thirty-sixth chapter, speaking of Jesus Christ as "the high priest of our offerings, the defender and helper of our weakness" (36.1; cf. 61.3), and may even echo Hebrews 1:3 with the words "through him we fix our gaze on the heights of heaven, through him we see the reflection of his faultless and lofty countenance" (36.2), there is no trace at all of the notion that through the Son God made the ages (Heb. 1:2). In the final prayer to the Father, Jesus Christ is called the "beloved child" of God, as in the *Didache*.[1] The Master of spirits and Lord of all flesh is said to have "selected" Jesus, not "generated" him (64). Presumably Clement is not acquainted with Gnostic ideas about creation or the sonship of Christ or, for that matter, with the Gospel of John.

Hermas

Also from Rome we have the *Shepherd* of Hermas with its Visions, Commandments, and Similitudes. Hermas never mentions Jesus or Christ. (In such silence he joins the *Epistle to Diognetus,*[2] Tatian, Theophilus, and even Minucius Felix.) Instead, his first "commandment" requires belief "that God is one, who made all things and perfected them, and made all things for existence out of the non-existent and contains all, alone himself uncontained." On the other hand, in the ninth Similitude (12.2–3) we learn that "the Son of God is older than all his creation, so that he was the counselor of his creation to the Father," and was also manifested at the end of the last days. He can be identified with the Spirit (5.6.5, 9.1.1). In the eighth Similitude a great willow tree is identified as God's law, which in turn is identified as God's Son, while an angel who prunes the tree is the archangel Michael, who puts the law into the hearts of believers (8.3.2–3). It seems clear that Hermas (whether one author or several) is no theologian. His vigorous monotheism makes difficulties for his Christology. In the second Vision we read that "God has sworn by his Son that those who have denied their Lord have been rejected from their life" (2.2.8), but there is no explanation of who Son or Lord are.

It would be odd if Hermas had taught at Rome along with Justin. The Muratorian list makes Hermas contemporary and indeed the brother of Pius, bishop at that time. Fortunately, however, Professor A. C. Sundberg, Jr., has shown that the fragment provides fourth-century fantasy, not second-century information.[3] It is likely, then, that he wrote very early in the second century or even at the end of the first.

What Clement and Hermas say, and especially what they do not say, indicates that Christological speculation was not prominent in Christian thought at Rome in the early second century.

Ignatius of Antioch

At Antioch, however, the Syrian bishop Ignatius was setting forth "an informal confession" resembling the older apostolic preaching or the later declaration underlying the

Apostles' Creed. The most complete of the examples cited by J. N. D. Kelly[4] is this:

> Be deaf when anyone speaks to you apart from Jesus Christ, who was of the stock of David, who was from Mary, who was truly born, ate, and drank, was truly persecuted under Pontius Pilate, was truly crucified and died in the sight of beings heavenly, earthly, and under the earth, who also was truly raised from the dead, his Father raising him.

Ignatius also insisted that Jesus Christ should be called "our God"; he is

> both flesh and spirit, born and not born, God in man, true life in death, both from Mary and from God, first passible and then impassible, Jesus Christ our Lord.
>
> *To the Ephesians* 7.2

Ignatius claims that Jesus truly suffered and boldly refers to "the suffering of my God" (Rom. 6.3). He denounces those who like the Gnostics hold a contrary view and reiterates the paradox of the incarnation. "Wait for him who is . . . timeless, invisible, intangible, impassible." These are the conventional divine attributes that both Ignatius and the Gnostics ascribed to Christ. He went farther, however, when he added that this divine Christ "for us was visible, for us accepted suffering, in every way enduring for us" (*Polyc.* 3.2).

Ignatius must have known that not all Christians accepted such formulations, for in his letters to the Magnesians and the Philadelphians, congregations that were fairly close to Judaism, he does not speak of Jesus as God. In Magnesians, however, he does refer to Jesus Christ as "before the ages with the Father" (*Magn.* 6.1) and as God's "Logos proceeding from silence" (8.2).

Ignatius thus takes a significant step in the development of doctrine, for he insists upon the reality of Christ as both God and human and upon his role in both creation and redemption. To be sure, as a prospective martyr writing to congregations on unity, he does not explain his paradoxes. By maintaining them in the face of opposition, chiefly Gnostic, he preserved the basic materials for a doctrine so that later generations could work out the difficulties, or at least work on them. His younger colleague Polycarp was no theologian, but he too insisted on the reality of Christ's coming "in the flesh" (7.1)[5] and holding after Ignatius that Jesus had "endured everything for us" (8.1).

Both *Barnabas* and *2 Clement* are attentive to other doctrines, though Barnabas does say that God spoke to the Lord as he was creating humankind (5.5, 6.12), and that it was this same Lord who suffered. The anonymous sermon called *2 Clement* begins thus: "We must think of Jesus Christ as of God" but does not identify Jesus Christ as God in the manner of Ignatius. It too speaks of the "great sufferings Jesus Christ endured for us" (1.1–2). It thus contains some ingredients of Christological thought, but its author is chiefly concerned with morality, not a doctrine of Christ.

The same observation could be made in regard to all the writings of the apostolic fathers. There is nothing complete, shaped, logically significant about their Christologies. Each one seems to be trying to express either a personal conviction or the faith of a local church. They are quite different from the Gnostics, who apparently start with their special mythologies, take aspects of Christological texts from the Bible, and build systems out of them. More orthodox Christians were not ready to argue with the Gnostic teachers before the time when apologetic theologies arose.

Defenses Against Gnosticism

It is hard to tell how successfully the apostolic fathers opposed Gnosticism and other heresies, though the survival of their writings shows that something was being achieved. When Ignatius of Antioch denounced Docetists, he did so in Asia Minor, far from his native Antioch, and it is hard to tell what effect his complaints had in Syria itself. The church at Rome did not finally confront the Gnostic problem until the year 144, when its presbyters finally expelled Marcion from the community. For a decade thereafter there was confusion over the books of the developing Christian canon. Justin, writing around 157, was still unable to cite the epistles of Paul or even mention the apostle, and while he knew the Gospel of John he could not refer to it. Presumably Polycarp, who visited Rome shortly before his martyrdom, was able to speak there of "the blessed and glorious Paul" and encourage study of his letters (*Phil.* 3.2). He certainly attacked any Gnostic who denied the future resurrection and judgment and called such a person, like Marcion, "Satan's firstborn" (7.1). As he had reminded the Philippians of the endurance of Ignatius and Paul (9.1), so now he must have recalled it again. Even though Valentinians and other Gnostics were still active in Rome, Polycarp brought many of them back to the church.[6]

During and after the Gnostic crisis at Rome the church's leaders insisted more firmly on ideas about apostolic faith handed down by apostolic ministers in apostolic tradition as found in apostolic books. At any rate, this is what Irenaeus indicates: at Rome Polycarp proclaimed that "from the apostles he had received only a single and unique truth and had transmitted it to the church." In other words, apart from learned debate many Christians were recognizing the importance of their own traditions. The point was important since not long afterward Ptolemaeus wrote his *Letter to Flora* and insisted that Valentinians too had received the apostolic tradition by succession.[7] Around the time when Polycarp visited Rome, a Gnostic teacher named Marcellina arrived with the traditions and permissive morality of Carpocrates and won many adherents.[8] The church had to set forth its tradition in a simple and persuasive manner.

Justin's Traditional Doctrine

Justin repeatedly describes the tradition about Christ as he has received it. As Kelly points out, it was "a simple Christological kerygma,"[9] with a setting in baptism and eucharist. He speaks of worshiping the Father and also "Jesus Christ, who was crucified under Pontius Pilate. . . . He is the Son of the true God" (*Apology* 1.13.3). In addition, he tells of bap-

tism "in the name of Jesus Christ, who was crucified under
Pontius Pilate" (61.13). Such confessions, or baptismal answers, point toward the Apostles' Creed with its summary of
the apostolic preaching.

As an older contemporary of the Gnostic Valentinus, Justin belonged to a very different kind of community at Rome.
Like Gnostic leaders he headed his own school, but he stood
much closer to the general run of Christians and their traditions, since for him the common faith was expressed in the
common eucharist to which he referred several times. In the
Dialogue he mentions[10]

> the bread of the eucharist, which Jesus Christ our Lord com-
> manded us to offer for the remembrance of the passion which
> he suffered for those whose souls are cleansed from all wicked-
> ness; so that we might give thanks to God not only for his cre-
> ation of the world with everything in it for the sake of humanity
> but also for having freed us from the wickedness in which we
> had lived and for having completely destroyed the principali-
> ties and powers through him who became passible in accord-
> ance with his will.

Clearly this is an expression and explanation of the common
faith and practice to which Justin adheres.

The common faith is also expressed in the semicreedal
statements that Justin occasionally supplies. "We revere and
worship the true God and the Son who came from him and
taught us these things . . . " (*Apology* 1.6.2) and "We honor
him who has taught us these things and was born for this purpose, Jesus Christ, who was crucified under Pontius Pilate,
the governor of Judaea in the time of Tiberius Caesar, having
learned that he is the Son of the true God" (1.13.3). More specifically, the language is baptismal and therefore traditional.
Baptism, Justin says, is "in the name of Jesus Christ, who
was crucified under Pontius Pilate" (1.61.13). J. N. D. Kelly
cites eight examples of "a simple Christological kerygma"
that must be "echoes of the liturgy or teaching of the
church."[11] Five of the eight also refer to Christ's birth from
Mary.

Justin thus begins with the *incarnate* Son of God, not philosophical speculation about creation or redemption. This incarnate Son was specifically the Jesus Christ of the Synoptic Gospel traditions, and Justin's insistence on the point later made him Irenaeus' favorite apologist. He explains that Christians take their name from "our teacher Jesus Christ, who is the Son and messenger of God the Father and Master of all" (*Apology* 1.12.9).[12] They revere God and his Son and the army of the other good angels who follow him and are like him, as well as the prophetic Spirit (1.6.2). Historians have worried about the army of angels, but Justin soon rephrases his Three, calling them "the Creator of all and, in the second place, our teacher Jesus Christ, crucified under Pontius Pilate, Son of the real God, and in the third rank the prophetic Spirit" (13.3). In any case, the angels belong to the army of which the Logos is the chief general (cf. *Dialogue* 61.1). Justin is not greatly concerned with the philosophical problems of incarnation.

In fact, what seems to have troubled him most was the resemblance of the gospel story to myths about Greek gods, though he tries to turn it into a defense of the gospel.

> When we say that the Logos, the first begotten by God, was born without sexual intercourse as Jesus Christ our teacher, and that he was crucified and died and rose again to ascend into heaven, we bring forward nothing new in comparison with those whom you call sons of Zeus.[13]

Justin proceeds to provide an exercise in comparative religion. Hermes like Jesus was the hermeneutical Logos and teacher of all; Asclepius was another healer who, though killed, ascended into heaven; while Dionysus was torn asunder, and Heracles in flight from pain gave himself to the fire. Justin derides the ascended gods known from the merely conventional names of constellations and ridicules people who swear they have seen deceased emperors riding off into the sky. In turn, a decade later the Roman prefect Rusticus would ridicule Justin's own expectation of ascending to the sky: "If you are scourged and beheaded, do you believe you will ascend to heaven?" Perhaps he had read the *Apology*.

After deriding the behavior of the gods, especially Zeus and his sons, he calls them evil demons, not gods, but again notes the similarities in question, this time adding Perseus born of a virgin and Asclepius working cures like those of Jesus. "But Jesus Christ alone was truly born to God as a son, since he was his Logos and Firstborn and Power, and by God's will he became man and taught us these things for the conversion and restoration of the human race."[14]

Justin has to discuss these gods because of his emphasis on the Jesus of Christian tradition, who really lived, died, and rose—and was predicted in the Old Testament. In other words, his emphasis on the reality of Jesus leads him to a kind of biblical theology. To prove that Jesus was not like the sons of Zeus and was not a magician, he goes through Old Testament predictions pointing to Christ and devotes nearly half his *Apology* (chapters 30–60) to this effort. A Roman emperor, or even a secretary dealing with petitions, was not likely to find this kind of material convincing or impressive. It meant more within the Christian community and especially for Justin himself, who had been converted by encountering the Old Testament prophets (*Dialogue* 7). He adds that Jesus called himself "Son of Man" either because of his birth through a virgin or because he was descended from David and the patriarchs (100.3). Any apocalyptic overtone has disappeared.

The Generation of Sophia or Logos

The simple confession we have described was not the only foundation of Justin's teaching about Christ. There was another side to it, theologically more creative: his development of a Logos doctrine that in essence can be traced back to the apostle Paul and his words about Wisdom in 1 Corinthians 8:6, as well as to the Johannine Logos.

In his earlier *Apologies* Justin does not explicitly mention Sophia ("Wisdom") as God's agent in creation and revelation. He prefers the Johannine and semiphilosophical term *Logos,* and says of wisdom only that "because of *sophia* Jesus was worthy to be called Son of God" (*Apology* 1.22.1). This must be Jesus' own wisdom, occasionally mentioned in the Synoptic Gospels. On the other hand, he implicitly refers to Proverbs when he says that the Logos was the "first thing generated by God" (1.21.1; cf. 33.6).

In the more fully developed *Dialogue,* however, Justin relies on Proverbs 8:22–36 to show that God generated a certain rational (*logikē*) power out of himself as a "beginning" before all created beings. In scripture, Justin says, the Holy Spirit calls this power "Glory of the Lord," "Son," "Sophia," "Angel," "God," "Lord," and "Logos," and the Logos called it "Chief General" when appearing in human form (Josh. 5:14).[15] If the Logos is "Chief General" and "Angel," it must be general of an army of angels, as in Justin's view it is. The Logos is therefore present throughout the Old Testament revelation. While it is inseparable from the Father, when the Father wills, God makes it "leap forth" or withdraws it to himself (123.3).

In order to explain the generation of the Logos Justin uses human and natural analogies already employed by Middle Platonists like Philo and Numenius. The Logos originates as human speech does: when we emit a word (*logos*), we generate it and do not emit it by abscission (*kata apotomēn*) as if the reason (*logos*) in us were diminished. Similarly one fire can be lighted from another (61.2)[16] or light from light (128.3).

It is not clear exactly how the idea that "the seed of the Logos was implanted in every race of men" is related to these analogies. The examples Justin gives are the philosophers Heraclitus and Musonius Rufus (*Apology* 2.8.1) and apparently also Socrates (1.5.3–4; cf. 2.10.8). It may be significant that Justin, who regarded both Socrates and Heraclitus as Christians (1.46.3), himself became a Christian once a fire was lighted in his soul (*Dialogue* 8.1).

As for the terms "seed of the Logos" and "spermatic Logos" (*Apology* 2.8.3, 13.1), they may come from Stoic philosophy, in which the term was used to explain the divine origin of life and motion in matter.[17] (These precise terms are hard to find in Middle Platonism.) Chrysippus claimed that matter (Hera) received the spermatic logoi of Zeus (God) and thus became a cosmos.[18] Justin used the term not for cosmology but for showing how sages could agree with the moral teaching of the incarnate Logos without knowing it directly. His basic point was that "whatever all have said well belongs to us Christians" (2.13.4; cf. 10.2). This point had been made by the Stoic Seneca to justify his use of Epicurus, and Justin's language is close to Seneca's: "The best ideas are common property" and "whatever is well said by anyone is mine."[19] Presumably Justin did not use Seneca; the thought was commonplace, and Clement used it to explain what he meant by philosophy.[20] In general, Justin's ideas do not reflect a specifically philosophical milieu.[21]

In fact, his basic idea about the Logos comes from John, as the following three texts prove. First, Justin says that the Logos, the "seed from God," is the Son of God, and he promises to tell how he "was *made incarnate and became man*" (*Apology* 1.32.8–10; John 1:14). Second, the eucharistic bread and wine become "the *flesh and blood* of that *incarnate* Jesus" (66.2; John 1:14, 6:53). Third, Jesus was "the *only-begotten of the Father* of all (especially Father of his *Logos* and Power) and later became man [John 1:14] through the virgin, as we learned from the reminiscences (of the apostles)" (*Dialogue* 105.1).

When we take these three passages into account, we gain a clearer impression of the statement about baptism in *Apology* 1.61.4–5. "Christ said, 'Unless you are reborn, you will not enter into the kingdom of the heavens.' It is obvious to all that it is impossible for men once born to enter into their mothers' wombs." Clearly this is a rather close citation of John 3:3–4, with *anōthen*, "anew" or "again" or possibly "from above," omitted because according to Justin's understanding of the word it would be either tautological or meaningless. In addition, he rephrases John's expression "kingdom of God," which he himself never uses. The passage thus reinforces our belief that the theology of John, like the exegesis of Paul, underlies much of Justin's thought,[22] even though he never names, or quotes from, either author. (Presumably both were controversial in his time.)

When Justin argues against Jewish monotheists in the

Dialogue, he insists that there is a "second God" (as Philo had suggested) and that this is Christ.[23] The supreme God is "Lord of the Lord on earth, since he is Father and God and the cause for the existence of the Mighty One, Lord, and God" (129.1). Verbally, we are again in the realm of Numenius, who spoke of a First God, a Second, and a Third, and sometimes assimilated the Third to the Second.[24] Even in Justin's thought the Second and the Third seem sometimes identified, as when he speaks of the conception of Jesus by a "spirit and power from God, none other than the Logos" (*Apology* 1.33.6). We shall discuss this passage below.

But while Justin may be indebted again to Numenius for some important phrasing used in his theology, the doctrines as such come from the Christian exegetical tradition. The Logos is inseparable from the Father but numerically distinct, for in Genesis 3:22 we read, "Behold, Adam has become like one of us"; and Wisdom, distinct from her Father, says in Proverbs 8:21 (in Greek), "I will tell you things forever numbered" (*Dialogue* 129.2–3).

In other words, some striking language and analogies may well come from contemporary philosophy, probably from Numenius of Apamea. Justin's basic doctrine of Christ, however, is based on Christian tradition. At this point his ideas are different from those of the later apologist and bishop Theophilus, who attacked philosophers more vehemently but conceded much more to them, as well as to the Jewish Christianity that Justin tolerated but did not regard as fully orthodox (*Dialogue* 45–47). Perhaps Theophilus was really addressing Jewish Christians or even Jews, but Justin, ostensibly addressing Roman emperors, tried to refute both Jewish exegesis of the Old Testament and pagan criticism of Christians.

The Conception of Jesus

Justin's ideas about the conception of Jesus may seem surprising. As J. N. D. Kelly put it, "It is noteworthy that Justin did not assign the Holy Spirit any role in the incarnation." "Like other pre-Nicene fathers he understood the divine

Spirit and power of the Most High mentioned in Luke 1:35 not as the Holy Spirit but as the Logos."[25] We might imagine that Justin had forgotten that both Matthew 1:18, 20 and Luke 1:35 point to the Holy Spirit as the agent of conception, though in Luke's infancy narrative so much is ascribed to the Spirit[26] that the angel's prediction in 1:35 might not seem distinctive enough. Certainly Ignatius spoke of Jesus the Christ as "conceived by Mary by the dispensation of God, of the seed of David and of the Holy Spirit" (*Eph.* 18.2), but he could also say, less specifically, that he was "of the family of David according to the flesh, Son of God by the will and power of God" (*Smyrnaeans* 1.1). When Justin quotes Luke 1:35 he mentions not the Spirit but the Power that "overshadowed" Mary, and goes on to lay emphasis on the Holy Spirit in a paraphrase of Matthew 1:20–22 (1.33.4–5). These passages reflect an ambiguity that appears in Justin's own conclusion. "It is right to regard the Spirit and the Power from God[27] as none other than the Logos, who is also the first born of God as Moses the prophet signified" (1.33.6). In the *Dialogue,* however, Justin's language about the birth is highly figurative. He imagines that the virgin Eve conceived "the word [*logos*] from the serpent and bore disobedience and death," while the Virgin Mary, addressed by the angel, responded, "Let it be to me according to your word [*rhēma*]" (100.5). Even so, it looks as though his ideas were becoming more biblical, since elsewhere in the *Dialogue* he quotes Matthew 1:18–20 to show that Mary conceived "by the Holy Spirit" (78.3).

Toward the Nicene Creed

The movement toward speculative analysis reflected in Justin's Christology flourished in Christian churches even after the Gnostic crisis faded away. Some authors simply repeated what Justin and others had said or unduly emphasized parts of their teaching and thus led to incomplete formulations. Others continued to work in the spirit of the apologists and within the church; Athanasius is a symbol of their work.

We have suggested that the Apostles' Creed reflects the apostolic preaching with its emphasis on the humanity of Jesus. On the other side, there seems to be a rather full statement about his divinity in the Nicene Creed, following the line begun in 1 Corinthians 8:6 and the Johannine prologue and related to Justin's fundamental statements made in the mid-second century.

The words "And in one Lord Jesus Christ" exactly echo the phrase in 1 Corinthians, while the terms related to the generation of the Son of God reflect what John and Justin said.[28] Other sections reflect fourth-century disputes; these include "true God from true God" (cf. John 17:3); "begotten not made"; and "*homoousios* with the Father." We return to the New Testament and, of course, to Justin with the statement about creation through the Logos or Son: "Through whom all things were made."[29] And for the incarnation we find a synthesis of John and Luke that Justin could easily have provided had he thought about the question more intently. "Who for us men and for our salvation came down from heaven [John 3:13] and became incarnate [John 1:14] by the Holy Spirit of the Virgin Mary [Luke 1:35] and was made man."

But we shall see that not every Christian accepted Justin's positions or the statements made in the creed.

5

The Jewish Christian Christology of Theophilus

Justin Martyr's rather simple apologetic provided clear and traditional statements of second-century Christology. Since he quoted neither the Pauline epistles nor the prologue to John, his theological task was easier than it might have been. His successors faced greater difficulty partly because they used more New Testament texts and partly because they went farther into rhetoric, philosophy, and pagan theology. Melito of Sardis, for example, loved gaudy rhetoric, and it allowed him such a paradox as "God has been murdered." This was a problem, not a solution, though an anonymous author later praised him for speaking of Christ as God and human. Melito's contemporary Athenagoras discussed the Trinity and used syllogisms to prove the unity of God. He was unable, however, to say anything about the incarnation. Tatian mentioned "the God who suffered" but did not name Jesus, though he too was cited by the anonymous author as speaking of Christ as God.[1]

A very different kind of Christology appears in the writings of Theophilus of Antioch, apologist, exegete, and bishop. His views will seem strange, but we recall that in his time there was wide diversity over this doctrine even at Rome. There Theodotus of Byzantium identified Jesus as a man who was born of a virgin and worked miracles after the Christ, the Spirit "in the form of a dove" (Luke 3:22), entered him. He became God either when the Spirit descended or after he rose plicitly Christian than those of his apologetic predecessor Justin. Theophilus uses the language of Job and the Psalms to depict the wonders of creation but never refers to redemption or, indeed, to the eucharist as such. Such silences suggest that he is on the borderline between Christianity and Judaism, if, indeed, there was a clear line between the two in his mind.

Theophilus also sets forth a rather extreme doctrine of God's transcendence, first claiming positively that God is supreme in glory, greatness, height, strength, wisdom, goodness, and beneficence. Next he takes a list of thirteen appellations of God, chiefly from the New Testament, and claims that each refers merely to divine aspects or attributes, not to God per se (1.3). The reason he does so seems to appear toward the end. "If I call him Fire, I speak of his anger. Doubtless you will ask, 'Is God angry?' Certainly: he is angry with those who do evil deeds, but good and gentle and merciful [Exod. 34:6] for those who love and fear him" (1.3). Presumably Theophilus is countering the attack of the Marcionites such as Apelles, who listed twenty-three examples of God's moral delinquency from the Pentateuch.[15] (Theophilus attacks Apelles in 2.25–27.) His doctrine of transcendence will make it hard to speak of incarnation.

Theophilus' Doctrine of Sophia and Logos

Certainly Theophilus follows New Testament writers and other Hellenistic Jews who spoke of God's Wisdom (Sophia) and Word (Logos). Sometimes he treats them separately (1.7), sometimes as the two hands of God (2.18). In his second book he goes on to identify them with each other—and with other divine powers or attributes as well (2.10, 22). The doctrine is rather unstable, though perhaps he is following Philo, who once stated that Eden meant the Sophia of God and added that it was also God's Logos.[16] He may also be combining ideas from Paul, who called Christ Wisdom, and John, who called him Word.

Unfortunately he tries to coordinate all the titles. Logos is equivalent to Spirit, Beginning, Wisdom, and Power of the Most High (Spirit in Luke 1:35) (2.10). Logos is the Power and the Sophia of God (1 Cor. 1:24) and God's Son, Mind, and Intelligence (2.22). We might hope that Sophia would be the Logos while within God and Logos would be Sophia when expressed, for Theophilus says that Sophia was in God and Logos was always with God, but he says that God generated both. Perhaps he is following something like the Palestinian Targum to Genesis, which begins thus: "From the beginning, the Word of Yahweh, with Wisdom, created and completed the heavens and the earth."[17] Once more his doctrine finds a Jewish setting.

Sophia and Logos have the same basic functions. God created the universe through Sophia (1.7; 2.10, 22). She named the stars, inspired the prophets, and created fish and birds (1.6; 2.9, 12, 16). Theophilus also refers to her as God's "offspring" (*gennēma*), clearly pointing toward Proverbs 8:25 as the source of his ideas. By retaining both Logos and Sophia and neglecting the terms Father, Son, and Spirit, Theophilus produced a considerable measure of confusion, which Irenaeus endeavored to correct (chapter 7).

The Generation of the Logos

Two key passages express what Theophilus thought about the generation of the Logos. The first passage (2.10) introduces exegesis of the opening books of Genesis by summarizing what the prophets taught about creation. This was the primary teaching of "the divine Scripture."

> God, having his own Logos innate [*endiatheton*] in his own bowels [*splanchna*], begot him, together with his own Sophia, by "vomiting him forth" [Ps. 45:1] before everything else. . . . He is called "Beginning" [John 1:1] because he leads and dominates everything fashioned through him. It was he, "Spirit of God" [Gen. 1:2] and "Sophia" [Prov. 8:22] and "Power of the Most High" [Luke 1:35], who came down into the prophets and spoke through them. . . . They did not exist when the world came into existence; there were the Sophia of God which is in

Logos as Thought and Word

The other passage on the generation of the Logos occurs at the end of Theophilus' commentary on the creation story (2.22). Here the language used has fewer mythological overtones but still reflects ideas like those of the Stoic Chrysippus on the way the Logos was "expressed," as we have already seen.

> God's Logos, through whom he made everything, who is his Power and Sophia [1 Cor. 1:24], assumed the role of the Father and Lord of the universe, was present in paradise in the role of God and conversed with Adam. The divine scripture itself teaches us that Adam said he "heard the voice." What is the Voice but the Logos of God, who is also his Son?

At this point Theophilus retells the story of the generation of the Logos in different language, emphasizing another aspect of Psalm 45:1.

> The Logos was always innate in the Heart [Ps. 45:1] of God. Before anything came into existence he had him as his Counsellor, his own Mind and Intelligence [*phronēsis*]. When God wanted to make what he had planned to make, he generated this Logos, making him *external,* as the Firstborn of all creation [Col. 1:15]. He did not deprive himself of Logos but generated the Logos and constantly converses with his Logos [citing John 1:1a–b]. Originally God was alone and the Logos was in him.[29]

To prove his point Theophilus then cites John 1:1c–3, which many early exegetes understood thus (cf. chapter 2).

He follows Justin (*Dialogue* 128.3) in describing the function of the Logos as God's messenger.

> Since the Logos is God and derived his nature from God, whenever the Father of All wills to do so he sends him into some place where he is present and is heard and seen [cf. 1 John 1:1]. He is sent by God and is recognized as being in a place.

The notion that a thought begins in the heart, proceeds to the head, and then is emitted as speech is commonplace in Hellenistic thought, though Chrysippus set forth the idea with special force.[30] Presumably he was the philosophical authority on whom Theophilus relied for both pictures of the generation from internal to external.

Philo too differentiated human thought, the internal logos, from its expression in speech, the external logos,[31] but Theophilus was the first to apply the terms to the divine Logos. Irenaeus vigorously denounced anthropomorphism of this sort and attacked Gnostics who placed their aeons "in the viscera of the Father,"[32] and Origen returned to Philo's position and admitted the distinction only for human psychology.[33] Eusebius attacked Marcellus of Ancyra for discussing the origin of the Logos in language like that of Theophilus.[34]

The Logos in Eden and After

However the Logos came forth, it was the agent of creation and later appeared in Eden, as both Philo and Justin had stated. In Genesis 3:10 Adam said he heard the voice of God who was walking in paradise, and since God cannot be present in a particular place, this Voice must have been God's Logos. The Logos was "assuming the role" (*analambanōn to prosōpon*) of God. Presumably Theophilus did not consider Christological implications but simply gave exegesis of Genesis 3:8, where Adam and Eve hid from the *prosōpon* or "face" of God. Other exegetes dealt with the "face" of God in more detail. Philo explicitly stated that God has no face.[35] A Christian interpretation develops in Irenaeus[36] and Clement of Alexandria, both of whom identified God's "face" as the Logos.[37] Apparently Theophilus was not concerned with such details.

For Theophilus as for his predecessors the Logos (or Sophia, or Spirit) inspired the prophets. God sent *them* (not one, as in Deuteronomy 18:15) "from among *their* brothers" to "teach and remind" the people of the Mosaic law (3.11). According to John 14:26 the Paraclete, the Holy Spirit, will "teach and remind" Christians of everything Jesus said to his disciples. These allusions suggest that for Theophilus, Jesus repeated the law of Moses in a stricter form (3.13). In any event, the Old Testament law agrees completely with the prophets and the Gospels (3.9–14). For Theophilus, as for his Jewish Christian contemporary Hegesippus, the ultimate authorities for Christian life and doctrine were "the law and the prophets and the Lord."[38]

The Role of Jesus

The most surprising feature of Theophilus' theology, noted already, is his complete silence in regard to Jesus and his acts. Among the other early apologists, to be sure, Athenagoras and Tatian had just refrained from mentioning Jesus, while a little later Minucius Felix would offer even more mysterious silences.[39] Theophilus lays emphasis not on Jesus but on scripture, on God, God's Word and Wisdom, on creation and resurrection, and on baptism, churches, and heresies. His silence about Jesus might be due to apologetic convention, but more probably it is based on his peculiar doctrine about Christ.

All Theophilus could really say about Jesus is that he was born after the "Power of the Most High" came down upon Mary (Luke 1:35, alluded to in 2.10). Theophilus seems to believe in the virginal conception but not the incarnation. He thus resembles the adoptionist Theodotus of Byzantium, who taught that "Christ was a man like others but born of a virgin by the will of God when the Holy Spirit [or "Spirit of the Lord"] overshadowed her."[40] He used Luke's verses about the infant Jesus for his portrait of the infant Adam (2.24–25), and claimed that God gave Adam an "aptitude for progress (Luke 2:52) so that he might grow" in stature (Luke 1:80, 2:40) and thinking (equivalent to the "wisdom" of Luke 2:40, 52). In this context he used the expression "with God and men" (Luke 2:52) and spoke of human beings as "subject to parents" (Luke 2:51, 43)—though obviously neither statement could properly be made of Adam. There were no other humans in Adam's infancy, and he had no parents. Theophilus also notes that children must be obedient to God (cf. Luke 2:49), a point irrelevant to the early life of Adam, except insofar as Adam could be called "son of God" (Luke 3:38).

The language was especially meaningful for Theophilus because of its Old Testament and Jewish affinities. It meant that he could correlate the lives of Adam and Jesus and several other heroes of Israel. The language recalls the Old Testament pictures of Samson, Samuel, and David,[41] as well as Josephus' statements about Moses, Solomon, and indeed himself.[42] To be sure, such terms were not confined to Jewish circles, for a pagan inscription refers to a person who "was advancing in stature and proceeding toward piety."[43] Jews did use the language, however, and it is not very different from Paul's claims about his own youthful progress as a Jew (Gal. 1:14).

Adam was created neither mortal nor immortal but with two potentialities. If he had really progressed, he would have become "mature" or "perfect" (Eph. 4:13; cf. Matt. 5:48), would have been "declared a god," as Jesus was declared (John 20:28), and would have ascended into heaven, as Jesus did (Luke 24:52) (2.27). This picture implies that neither Adam nor Jesus was originally perfect.[44] Theophilus relies on the Jewish Christian doctrine of Christ as the Second Adam,[45] partly in agreement with 1 Corinthians 15:45–49 and Philippians 2:5–11 (he knows both letters) and partly in an even more Jewish manner. Nemesius of Emesa tells us that "the Jews say that man was created neither mortal nor immortal but in a state poised between the two."[46] This is Theophilus' doctrine.

Theophilus Against Paul

Another passage shows Theophilus revising Paul's comparison of Adam with Christ in order to contrast Adam in the past with humanity in the present—without any explicit reference to Christ.

To Autolycus 2.27	Rom. 5:15–21
What man acquired for himself through his neglect and disobedience, God now freely	Many died through one man's trespass The grace of God and the free

<for>gives him through love and mercy.	gift abounded for many
For as by disobedience *man* gained death for himself, so by obedience to the will of God	As by *one man's* disobedience many were made sinners so by *one man's* obedience

—now Theophilus begins to diverge rather sharply from Paul's Christological statement—

whoever will can obtain eternal life for himself.	many will be made righteous to eternal life.
For God gave us a law and holy commandments; *everyone* who does them can be saved and attaining to the resurrection can inherit imperishability.	7:12: the law is holy and the commandment is holy and just and good (cf. Gal. 3:12). 1 Cor. 15:50: inherit imperishability.

Theophilus insists that God will reward those who seek imperishability through good works[47] and strongly emphasizes justice as a virtue proclaimed by the prophets and the holy law of God.[48] (In his view Adam, Moses, Solomon, and probably Jesus himself were prophets.)[49] His Jewish Christian emphasis on obedience to the law of justice makes him view the work of Christ as exemplary, not efficacious. As in the Gospel of Luke, Christ's saving work disappears.[50] The doctrine of Irenaeus, as we shall see, is different,[51] but Origen and Nemesius agree that Adam could have become perfect by moral progress.[52]

In another passage, noted by Hitchcock, Theophilus rephrased Paul and, intentionally or not, minimized the saving work of Christ. In *To Autolycus* 2.1 he said Autolycus "supposed that our message was foolishness." Theophilus' "our message" replaces Paul's "message of the cross" (1 Cor. 1:18).[53]

Eusebius' Description of Ebionite Doctrine

What are we to conclude? Was Theophilus an Ebionite Christian? Certainly some features of Theophilus' teaching appear in Eusebius' account of Ebionite doctrine. "They held Jesus to be a plain and ordinary man who had achieved righteousness by moral progress [Luke 2:52] and had been born from the intercourse of Mary's husband with her," though "others did not deny that the Lord was born of a virgin and the Holy Spirit but, like the others, did not acknowledge his preexistence as God the Logos and Sophia." It is true that Theophilus said much about Logos and Sophia, but the question remains whether "the Lord" was preexistent as either one or both.

Both Ebionite groups held that "observance of the Law was essential, since they would not be saved merely through faith in Christ and life in accordance with this faith."[54] (That is, "the law ought to be kept in a more Jewish fashion.")[55] Therefore "they used to observe the Sabbath and the rest of the Jewish ritual, but on Sundays celebrated rites like ours in commemoration of the Savior's passion."[56] Here at least Theophilus is no Ebionite, for his Decalogue lacks the Sabbath commandment (3.9).

It must be admitted that Eusebius' account of Ebionite doctrine may not be fully historical. In a theological treatise he lumped Ebionites together with Paul of Samosata,[57] and he undoubtedly thought there were close resemblances. Is early Ebionite doctrine any more than a construct made by later antiheretical authors? In other words, did everyone who held some, or even all, the doctrines classified as Ebionite really belong to a definable party or sect? Perhaps the situation recalls various papal pronouncements on doctrines defined as Americanism or liberalism or modernism.

The Clementine Literature

It is odd that a certain Theophilus from Antioch appears in the Jewish Christian *Clementine Recognitions* (10.71) as donor of a large house to the community at Antioch. It is even more odd that many of Theophilus' ideas recur in the *Clementine Homilies* of uncertain date but certain unorthodoxy, where we find Adam identified with Christ and treated as the "true prophet" of the one God who created the world and will justly repay each person for his deeds (2.6,12). Adam was made by the hands of God and possessed the holy spirit of Christ (3.20). Those who criticize the Old Testament for its inadequate picture of God are ignorant of the interpolations in it. It was Jesus who explained that it is partly true, partly false. His expression "the truth of the scriptures," from their version of Matthew 22:29, proves that the scriptures are partly false and contain "interpolated" commandments about God's name and the Sabbath (3.49).

Conclusion

Though there are points at which Theophilus seems indebted to Ebionite doctrine, he was not an Ebionite himself. His picture of Jesus, however, is hard to coordinate with his doctrine of Logos and Sophia. If Jesus differed from others, it was in the obedience for which God finally gave him the name above every name and made him Lord and Christ (Phil. 2:8–9) or, indeed, God (2.27). Theophilus does refer to the Logos of God as "also his Son," but the Logos is preexistent, not incarnate (2.22). And while he does allude to a verse in Luke about the conception of Jesus (2.10), this goes no farther than Theodotus of Byzantium, who used the same verse.

At Antioch there was thus a sharp break between the incarnational Christology of Ignatius and the reticent monotheism of Theophilus. Who was to say that one was orthodox and the other not? Such problems, arising in very early times, were to plague the church at Antioch for many years. Serapion, bishop just after Theophilus, must have joined him in opposing Marcionites and supporting a Christianity closer to Judaism; he wrote that "we receive both Peter and the other apostles as Christ,"[58] thus using a Pauline phrase (Gal. 4:14) in support of the apostles whom Marcion had rejected. Paul of Samosata, bishop about seventy years later, shared many of Theophilus' ideas and was deposed by a synod of Origenist bishops from outside Antioch. He was so influential in the city, however, that the emperor Aurelian had to intervene in the case.[59]

We have analyzed Theophilus' Christology not to suggest that it was viewed as more or less orthodox than the views of other teachers in his time, but to show the startling diversity in Christological doctrines even toward the end of the second century. Presumably Christians at Antioch around 180 found Theophilus' teaching orthodox. It did justice to some aspects of New Testament thought and not to others, to Luke, for example, and not to Paul, but like complaints can be raised against most theologians. In the long run, however, a much stronger influence was exercised over the church by the more inclusive or catholic ideas of Irenaeus of Lyons, who will appear as our final second-century theologian.

6
Heresy and Christology

We have seen that among the Gnostics there were deviant in-terpretations of traditions ordinarily viewed as central. Un-fortunately not all bishops knew which interpretations to defend and which to reject. It appears that during Justin's early years some bishops of Rome could not identify Gnostic views as Gnostic, and for this reason Cerdo, Marcion, Valenti-nus, and Ptolemaeus flourished there. Irenaeus of Lyons had to write "letters against those in Rome who were falsifying the sound ordinance of the church," and Eusebius reports that Serapion, bishop of Antioch after Theophilus, was unable to detect the heresy latent in the apocryphal *Gospel of Peter*.[1]

Under such circumstances the definition of heresy in the antiheretical literature was a necessity. After Polycarp of Smyrna visited Rome and denounced Cerinthus, Marcion, and others,[2] Justin produced a treatise *Against All Heresies* there and perhaps included his earlier book *Against Mar-cion*,[3] if it was an independent work. Another bishop, Diony-sius of Corinth, wrote an anti-Marcionite letter.[4] Presumably each writer laid emphasis on themes he found especially con-genial. We know that Theophilus of Antioch, concerned with creation, wrote against the heretic Hermogenes, who held that God fashioned the world out of preexistent matter, and also attacked Marcion, obviously from his own Jewish Chris-tian standpoint.

An important recent study of heresy analyzes the works of

Justin, Hegesippus, and Irenaeus, to show how these writers developed the idea.[5] Earlier churchmen had opposed heresylike movements, as when Clement of Rome attacked "sedition" and upheld "apostolic succession" and Ignatius of Antioch denounced the heterodox; but Justin was the first to explain what heresy was and identify its manifestations. His work, echoed in his own *Apology* and used by Irenaeus, was more important than any other, for he knew something about the history of philosophy and used this knowledge to create an antiheretical framework. "Justin invented heresy."[6] Le Boulluec insists that he was vigorously Roman and agrees with Pierre Nautin that he created the early Roman episcopal succession list.[7] Certainly he took over the notion, fairly common in Platonists' debates, that a master's thought was preserved by some pupils but distorted by others, and directed it against heretics.

After Justin's time, Hegesippus came to Rome and fought heresy, relying largely on an episcopal succession list to cure it. What little of his doctrine remains seems isolated and rather provincial, and he contributed nothing to Christology.

Much more important was Irenaeus of Lyons, who used sources both heretical and antiheretical, made extensive use of rhetoric, and strongly insisted upon the unity of scripture (and its exegesis) and the unity of the church. He laid emphasis on apostolic succession while treating bishops as presbyers, and wrote especially against Valentinians (who also claimed apostolic succession) and Marcionites, heretics at Rome, whose heresies impressed him. Le Boulluec reasonably suggests that he wrote his major treatise just for the Roman church.[8] Like Justin he treated heresies genetically and refuted them by use of philosophy and rhetoric.

Was Rome the Citadel of Orthodoxy?

With this evidence for heresy as somehow related to Rome, we have to consider the thesis of Walter Bauer that the Roman church strongly defended "orthodoxy" and put down "heresy." Ever since the time of Paul it was clear that Rome was one of the greatest, probably the greatest, of churches. It lay on his missionary route to the West, and he counted on the Romans for support. According to Acts, he spoke like many a tourist or Roman provincial when he declared, "I must see Rome" (Acts 19:21). A generation later the Roman church had become stronger, and Clement of Rome wrote a letter in the church's name to Corinth in order to maintain law and order and prevent discord and rebellion. Was Clement concerned with heresy? Bauer claimed that he was because Irenaeus thought so.[9] Both Clement and Irenaeus wrote about dissension (*stasis*), however, not heresy.[10] Neither Paul's letter to the Romans nor *1 Clement,* therefore, gives reason to suppose that members of the early Roman church were unduly concerned with theological matters. Paul and Clement thought more about practical charity; some entered into slavery to ransom or provide food for others (*1 Clem.* 55.2). When Ignatius writes to Roman Christians, he urges them not to try to obstruct his impending martyrdom. He says not a word about the conflicts over doctrine which he emphasizes in his six other letters. Rome could hardly be described as a center of theological ferment.

A little later, the *Shepherd* of Hermas too suggests that doctrine was not supremely important in the Roman community. Personal asceticism and care for the poor were more immediate concerns. At the same time, Hermas does value inquiry about the deity and theological truth, and he knows "false prophets who corrupt the understanding of the servants of God." Though his test of truth is moral, not dialectical (*Mandates* 10–11), he insists at the beginning of the *Mandates* that belief in the one God, the Creator, is essential; accordingly, belief in many gods or in a god not the Creator is excluded. There is at least a hint of "orthodoxy against heresy"—that is, the Gnosticism of his time.

If this is how the theme developed, however, the Roman church certainly did not act as a doctrinal policeman at the beginning. Indeed, any such role was forced upon the leaders of the church by the Christians from elsewhere who brought their problems with them, around the middle of the second century, when various Gnostic teachers came to the city and made trouble among the relatively simple believers already there. Marcion's predecessor Cerdo arrived sometime in the 130s, perhaps from Syria, and taught a dualistic theology that naturally resulted in difficulties wherever Hermas' axiom was accepted. Irenaeus' account of Cerdo suggests that he drifted in and out of church, teaching dualism sometimes in secret, sometimes in public. Perhaps in 137, his admirer Marcion arrived from Pontus and gave the church a large sum of money in order to win friends. His money and literary skill did not outweigh a lopsided theology, however, and in 144 a group of presbyters finally excommunicated him and returned his donation.

Since his arrival at Rome coincides rather closely with the "accession" of Hyginus (about whom we know nothing), and his departure took place shortly after Hyginus' death, there was probably a good deal of conflict related to this bishop and his relations with Marcion, who could even have been his protégé. Irenaeus tells us that the heretic Valentinus also came to Rome under Hyginus.[11] Both he and Marcion were closer to Christianity, orthodox or not, than most other Gnostics, and this may explain why Hyginus, unlike his successors, was maintaining a conciliatory attitude. In addition, the government of the church by a college of presbyters, mentioned by both Hermas and Epiphanius, does not point to a strong episcopate.

Pius was bishop after Hyginus and held office for fifteen years about which we know little. His successor Anicetus showed more concern for episcopal order, for tranquillity, and for cooperation with such visiting bishops as the Asian Polycarp, whom he allowed to celebrate the Easter eucharist on the Asian date, not the Roman one, maintaining cordial relations with him. Irenaeus tells how it took Polycarp to restore many followers of Marcion and Valentinus to the church.[12]

Orthodoxy and Heresy in Justin

Justin may well have written his apology a year or two after Polycarp's visit and soon after his martyrdom in Asia. The presence of visitors like this, not to mention the many whose names we do not know, must have increased doctrinal sensitivity even though some flexibility remained. The Roman church could not investigate every potentially heretical statement. Indeed, authors who in their way were orthodox to the core complained about the laxity of Roman bishops. Tertullian says that one of them almost admitted the right of Montanists to exist but then was dissuaded,[13] while the Roman Hippolytus claimed that both Zephyrinus (198–217) and Callistus (217–22), bishops of Rome at the beginning of the third century, were stupid or worse.[14] It is hard to see how Rome was doing much enforcing of orthodoxy. The Montanist Tertullian and the counter-bishop Hippolytus seem the most enthusiastic for rigor.

Where could Christians look for guidance on questions of orthodoxy and heresy? Under such circumstances the works of Justin and Irenaeus would be peculiarly helpful, for Justin insists upon his own "right-thinking," specifically in regard to apocalyptic eschatology.[15]

> I, and any other Christians who are right-thinking (*orthognō-mones*) in every respect, know that there will be a resurrection of the flesh and a thousand years to be spent in a Jerusalem built up and adorned and enlarged, as the prophets Ezekiel and Isaiah and the others acknowledge.

The thousand years, however, come not from these prophets but from the inspired John who wrote the Apocalypse, as he notes.[16] Justin is a good witness not for Rome's antiheretical "astuteness"[17] but for its conservative traditionalism.

Contrast with Rome's Later Situations

Romans were concerned with supporting other churches financially[18] on Roman charity and therefore took some interest in their correct beliefs. The Roman church was not likely to send funds to Gnostic groups or Montanists or extreme Judaizers. Inevitably, the church would try to find out who the recipients were, especially when some Roman Christians had sold themselves into slavery to ransom others. Under such circumstances the church might well have heeded the counsel of the *Didache*: "Let your alms sweat in your hands until you know to whom you are giving" (*Didache* 1.6).

In the third century Origen defended his own orthodoxy in letters to Fabian of Rome and other bishops as well,[19] while the Roman bishop was soon involved in the affairs of Carthage, Alexandria, and Antioch. Indeed, the Roman emperor Aurelian ordered the church building (*oikos*) at Antioch assigned to "those to whom the bishops of the doctrine [*dogma*] in Italy and the city of Rome would write letters" (7.30.19). By this time Roman orthodoxy had become more potent than in the second century.

Irenaeus' Idea of Consensus

Early in the reign of Commodus (180–92) Irenaeus wrote a defense and presentation of the theology he believed was or should have been Roman, perhaps for the Roman church where his influence had been significant for some years. The Gallican martyrs had recommended him to Eleutherius, bishop of Rome (175–89) (5.4.2), and in his treatise *On the Refutation and Destruction of Knowledge Falsely So-Called* he recognized Eleutherius' orthodoxy.[20]

In Irenaeus' view true orthodoxy is based on the apostolic faith as transmitted by bishops and presbyters in the worldwide church. His doctrine is one of *consensus*, common enough in antiquity and set forth in full clarity by Vincent of Lérins in the famous formula "everywhere, always, and by all." Vincent's *Commonitorium* clearly reveals the classical origin of his thought:[21] because exegetes are giving such diverse interpretations, scripture, the ultimate authority, is to be interpreted in the light of "the tradition of the Catholic church." What Vincent wants is "ecumenicity," "antiquity," and "consensio." There can be development in doctrine (*profectus*) but not alteration. Similarly Cicero had claimed that "by natural instinct we believe that gods exist, by reason we know what they are, and we think that souls continue on because of the *consensus* of all nations."[22]

explicitly of Paul as the author of epistles (in the plural) to Timothy and assigned a verse from Titus to him.[29] The intent of Theophilus and Irenaeus is much the same, but Irenaeus' citations are more precise.

Irenaeus probably rejected Hebrews,[30] even though it was known to Clement of Rome. While Eusebius says that in a lost work he mentioned and cited both Hebrews and the Wisdom of Solomon,[31] he need not have accepted either one. On the other hand, he certainly used 1 and 2 John, 1 Peter (as did his contemporaries Tatian and Theophilus), and possibly also James, Jude, and even 2 Peter. He definitely knew and used the Apocalypse of John, as did apologists from Justin onward. For him these documents were inspired and consistent witnesses to the revelation of God. With the Old Testament books, they were the primary authorities for the tradition.

The Apostolic Fathers

Irenaeus had no use for the apocryphal Christian literature often used at Alexandria and sometimes revered by modern scholars. Instead, he preferred the "apostolic fathers" later described by Eusebius and Photius. His usage is thus more Catholic and indeed more Roman than that of Alexandrian authors.[32] He refers to some of these fathers when he discusses apostolic and church tradition in Book 3, though he describes the letter of Clement of Rome (3.3.3) in terms taken almost entirely from the Bible, not *1 Clement* itself (except for emphasis on *stasis*). The description led C. Eggenberger to think he did not know the letter,[33] but Irenaeus was simply setting forth his own idea of orthodoxy. His ideas about succession seem to come from the letter. In the same context he refers to Polycarp's "most important letter" (3.3.4) and several chapters later paraphrases Ignatius' letter to Polycarp (3.16.6). Polycarp was especially important to him because he had known him personally and believed he was a link to the tradition of John at Ephesus.

In Book 4, when he begins to discuss creation, he appropri-

ately cites the *Shepherd* of Hermas, not naming the author
but backing him up by quotations from Malachi and Paul
(4.20.2). Later he takes Old Testament exegesis from an anonymous disciple of the apostles (4.27–32). In the fifth book,
where his theology seems somewhat more idiosyncratic, he
cites the martyr Ignatius, without naming him, on the importance of tribulation (5.28.4), as well as the millenarian teaching of Papias, who had seen and heard John, the Lord's
disciple (5.33.3–4). All these authorities stood near the beginning of the tradition.

Greek Apologists

Among the apologists, Irenaeus relied especially on Justin
and Theophilus because they wrote against heresy. He was
not interested in petitions to Roman emperors or defenses of
Christianity against its cultured despisers, for he was concerned specifically with theological teaching.

In his last two books, he twice cited the Roman theologian
Justin, once mentioning his treatise against Marcion: "Justin well says in his work *Against Marcion* that he would not
have believed the Lord himself if he had preached another
God beside the Creator" (4.6.2, 5.26.2). Justin had taught at
Rome and fought heresy there, and had taught Tatian for a
time.

Irenaeus also knew Tatian's *Oration* but despised its author as unorthodox. He believed that Tatian had kept the
faith only as long as he attended Justin's lectures but left the
church after his master's martyrdom. "Elated and inflated by
his claim to be a teacher, as if he were better than the rest, he
set up his own kind of doctrine." This is a not unfair summary of what Tatian said about himself in his *Oration,* and it
appears in the discussion of heresies in Irenaeus' first book
(1.28.1).

In the third book Irenaeus returned to the attack. "He invented <his teaching> on his own so that by introducing
something new in comparison with others, but speaking inani-
ties, he might acquire hearers devoid of faith while claiming to

be a teacher" (3.23.8). This description too is based on Tatian's own claims, for he said he had not been taught by anyone else and imagined that people were talking about the way he "made innovations beyond the infinite multitude of philosophers."[34] Irenaeus is repelled by an apologist who, though a disciple of a martyr-apologist, fell away from orthodoxy.

Irenaeus knew the apologist Theophilus of Antioch best of all. It may be that he realized his importance only gradually; most of his allusions occur in Books 4 and 5, though some come earlier.[35] He accepted parts of his theology but disliked his confused Christology. He revised Theophilus' analogies in the direction of simplicity, for example in his discussions of sense perception (1.2; *Heresies* 4.39.1) and vision (1.2; 4.29.1, 4.39.3), as well as the way in which the Spirit surrounds everything (1.5; 5.2.3).[36] We shall later see that he knew Theophilus' first two books but not the third, the only one to give a date in 180 or later.

Theophilus was certainly no absolute authority for him. Though he could have taken from Theophilus (1.4–5, 2.3) the doctrine that God contains all but is contained by none, he preferred the authority of Hermas (*Heresies* 4.20.1), whose writing he combined with the prophet Malachi and the apostle Paul.[37] But we shall discuss Irenaeus' relation to Theophilus more fully in chapter 7.

It is obvious that Irenaeus' idea of consensus is based on a rather thorough knowledge of basic Christian traditions before his time, notably in the New Testament and some of the apostolic fathers.

Consensus Built on Rome

Irenaeus presents a novel idea of exegetical and theological authority in the third book of his treatise. Significantly, it is preserved only in the Latin version. What he said was this:[38]

Ad hanc ecclesiam propter potentiorem principalitatem necesse est omnem convenire ecclesiam, hoc est eos qui sunt

undique fideles, in qua semper ab his qui sunt undique con-
servata est ea quae est ab apostolis traditio.

Which is to say:

> With this church, because of its more excellent origin, every
> church—that is, the believers from everywhere—must nec-
> essarily agree; this church in which the tradition from the
> apostles has always been preserved by those who are from ev-
> erywhere.

The statement is based on ideas of succession found in 1
Clement but goes beyond them. The apostolic tradition, correctly maintained at Rome, will solve all problems, and there
is no need for independent theological investigation.

Beyond Roman Consensus

Irenaeus' basic words about Rome do not appear in Eusebius' *Church History,* and the omission is important. We have
already noted that Irenaeus carries the Roman tradition up to
the time of Eleutherius but says nothing about his successor
Victor (189-98). The reason for this is clear enough: Victor
was locked in conflict with Polycrates, bishop of Ephesus,
precisely over the nature of apostolic tradition—the Asian
tradition with which Irenaeus had been brought up. Polycrates appealed to a succession of bishops reaching back to John
the Lord's disciple and refused to bend before Victor's threat
of excommunication. Irenaeus had to write Victor a defense of
toleration, reminding him how his predecessors had acted toward Asian customs.[39] We do not know how Victor responded.
The conflict gradually subsided, it seems. For our purposes,
the point must be clear: Irenaeus' idealistic view of the Roman episcopate as the basic authority was no longer viable.

An echo of this situation appears in what Roman Monar-
chians said about the tradition. They used Irenaeus' basic
outline to maintain that true apostolic orthodoxy had been
maintained at Rome up to the time of Victor and, apparently,
even under him. Under his successor Zephyrinus, however,

the truth was "counterfeited."[40] The difference between them and Irenaeus lay in their Adoptionist Christology.

The existence of conflicting traditions meant that simple appeals to "apostolic tradition" or to Rome lost their viability within Irenaeus' own lifetime. The appeals to tradition and authority ran into difficulties. Later on, at Carthage Tertullian would first reinterpret consensus as the ownership of the scriptures by the church and then turn to Montanism and individual interpretation. Even a devoted Romanist like Cyprian would eventually rewrite his treatise *On the Unity of the Catholic Church* so as to lay emphasis on the consensus of the whole episcopate, not on the primacy of the Roman bishop. The continuing problem is not our concern here, however, and we turn to Irenaeus' Christological contributions.

7

Irenaeus' Theology and Christology

Irenaeus of Lyons in Gaul is our final witness to second-century developments in Christology. He was a militant opponent of the Gnostics he had known in Asia Minor, probably at Rome, and certainly in Gaul itself. He was a devoted adherent of what he regarded as apostolic tradition, and had seen Polycarp of Smyrna, a living link to apostolic times. He was also rather better trained in philosophy than he admitted to his readers, and we shall see how boldly he innovated in doctrinal matters while claiming that his thought was traditional. In order to discuss Irenaeus and his Christology we must begin with his remarkable innovation in the doctrine of God.

Irenaeus' Doctrine of God

Much of Irenaeus' doctrine of God is based on biblical insights that the apologists often neglected, but as he combated Gnostic doctrines about emanations he used philosophical dogmas as well as biblical texts.[1] We shall see that he relied on Platonic sources, which in turn used the pre-Socratic philosopher Xenophanes.

Echoes of Xenophanes

Toward the end of the second century there was a renewed concern for the mysterious pre-Socratic philosophers and, indeed, for the history of philosophy in general; it is evident in the studies of Numenius and reflected in Justin's analysis of Christian heresies. The Skeptic Sextus Empiricus took pre-Socratic philosophers very seriously. Most of the fragments of Heraclitus come from citations in the second century and the early third, half of these made by the Christians Clement and Hippolytus. In addition, the thought of the pre-Socratics was revised and reinterpreted, for example in the first-century pseudo-Aristotelian treatise *On Melissus Xenophanes Gorgias,*[2] which may have influenced a Christian apologist. When Athenagoras argues in his *Embassy* (8) for the existence of only one god, he begins, "If there were two or more gods," thus repeating part of the argument assigned to Xenophanes in the treatise (977a25).[3] Athenagoras does not copy the treatise but seems to use it as a model. Only a few years later Irenaeus made frequent use of a genuine fragment from Xenophanes: God "wholly sees, wholly knows, and wholly hears."[4]

Irenaeus' context in his first citation (1.12.2) shows where he got it. He is contrasting the Lord of all, who "thinks and achieves at the same time, and wills and thinks at the same time," with the Zeus of Homer (*Iliad* 2.1-4), worried and sleepless as he plans to have many Greeks killed and honor the warrior Achilles. Irenaeus thus agrees with Xenophanes that God "effortlessly sets all things astir by the power of his mind alone,"[5] and shares his moral criticism of the poets: "Homer and Hesiod attributed many things to the gods that produce shame and blame for men, stealing and adultery and deceiving one another."[6] Critics of Homeric morality after Xenophanes complained not about *Iliad* 2.1-4 but about the verses immediately following (5-34), in which Zeus deceives the Greek leader Agamemnon with a dream of victory. Plato urged that God "is not the cause of all things, but only of the good," then denied that God deceives and denounced Homer's account of the dream.[7]

When Irenaeus criticizes Homer, he does not mention the dream, but he implies the Platonic criticism of it when he insists that God is the source of all good things (see below). It is, therefore, likely that he followed a Platonic source for theologi-

cal ideas ultimately derived from Xenophanes and his notion
that God is "wholly Thought [*cogitatus*], wholly Will, wholly
Mind, wholly Light, wholly Eye, wholly Hearing, wholly Source
of all good things."[8] While Theophilus of Antioch insisted on
the ineffability of God and claimed that such terms as Light,
Logos, Mind, and Spirit referred to divine activities, not to what
God is per se (1.3), Irenaeus' theology was more positive.

Further evidence to show that Irenaeus' intermediate source
was Platonic comes from three instances of the expression
"Source of all good things."[9] We have already noted its presence in Plato; it is also used by the Middle Platonists Philo
and Numenius[10] and repeated by the Platonizing Christians
Dionysius of Alexandria and Eusebius.[11] And when Irenaeus
claims that "religious men" use this statement about God
(2.13.3), he is referring to Platonists, for he applies the adjec-
tive to Plato himself, precisely because he called God just and
good (3.25.5). Indeed, he believes that the formulation also appears in the scriptures (2.28.4), perhaps because in Genesis 1:3
God spoke and light appeared. In his fourth book he uses the
formula again to support his own theory of development and
contrasts imperfect humanity, progressing and growing toward
God, with God himself, who is "perfect in every respect, equal
to and like himself, wholly Light, wholly Mind, wholly Substance, and the Source of all good things" (4.11.2).

In the first fragment of a spurious letter of Irenaeus to "De-
metrius, deacon of Vienne,"[12] the formula is echoed again:
"God is wholly Mind and Logos and Holy Spirit or Life."
While all the fragments contain theological ideas much later
than the second century, this much comes from Irenaeus—
and Xenophanes.

What Irenaeus sets forth is what he regards as taught by
"religious men" and the scriptures as well. In short, it is another expression of consensus.

Irenaeus' Christology

Irenaeus' innovative doctrine of God meant that he could
speak of Christ more positively than many of his predeces-

sors. On the one hand, in using Xenophanes' language about God's being "wholly" this or that, Irenaeus was making positive statements about God and thus avoided the theology of negation accepted by some of his contemporaries. On the other hand, the abstractness of Xenophanes' God meant that Irenaeus had to speak very concretely about the incarnate Son. Clement of Alexandria might apply Xenophanes' terms to the Son and call him "wholly Mind, wholly paternal Light, wholly Eye, seeing all, hearing all, knowing all,"[13] but Irenaeus insisted that Christ was the link between God and humanity. This, after all, is what he knew from the apostolic tradition, which guided his exegesis of the scriptures (4.36.2).

Irenaeus' Use and Correction of Theophilus

Given this strong doctrine of God's transcendence, Irenaeus had to link the Creator with the creation by taking over Theophilus' teaching about God's two "powers," Logos and Sophia. He states the basic idea in four passages: *Heresies* 3.24.2 and 4.20.2, 4 (all with references to Psalm 33:6), and *Demonstration* 10. These are based on Theophilus (1.7 and 2.18) and are explained in passages where Irenaeus identifies Logos as Son (2.30.9) and Sophia as (Holy) Spirit (4.7.4; 4.20.3). In another basic passage (4.20.1) Irenaeus follows Theophilus (1.7, 2.10) in quoting passages about Sophia from the book of Proverbs (3:19–20 and 8:22–25, 27–31). When he also quotes Psalm 33:6 several times for creation by Logos and Spirit and combines it with John 1:3,[14] the combination may come from Theophilus (1.7, 2.22).

Like Theophilus (1.5, 2.18), Irenaeus speaks of God's hands at work in creation, especially the creation of Adam.[15] But while Theophilus defined the "hands" as God's Logos and Sophia (2.18), Irenaeus is careful to identify them as Son and Spirit (4 preface 4; 5.6.1; 5.28.4) or Logos and Spirit (5.1.3) or to explain that Logos and Sophia are the same as Son and Spirit (4.7.4, 4.20.1).[16] He knows that the combination Son-Spirit is biblical, while Logos-Sophia is not. Logos and Sophia recur, though not as "hands," in the theology of Marcellus of Ancyra.[17]

Irenaeus explains, more carefully than Theophilus did, that the divine Triad is not really Father, Logos, and Sophia but Father, Son, and Holy Spirit. He turns back from the exaggerations of the apologists to the basic affirmations of the New Testament and the baptismal liturgy. Indeed, Theophilus had referred to the Son only once, stating that "the Logos of God is also his Son," generated as "the firstborn of all creation" (2.22; Col. 1:15), while elsewhere he identified the Logos with both Spirit and Sophia (2.10). Irenaeus is trying to overcome Theophilus' confusion of the divine persons. Later theologians who identified God's hands with divine persons took care to follow Irenaeus rather than Theophilus.[18]

The Generation of the Logos

Irenaeus is severely critical of Gnostic doctrine about the generation of the Logos.[19]

> If anyone asks us how the Son was emitted by the Father, we shall reply that no one knows about this emission or generation or enunciation or manifestation or whatever other name one wants to give this ineffable generation; not Valentinus, not Marcion, nor Saturninus nor Basilides nor angels nor archangels nor principalities nor powers, but only the Father who generated and the Son who was born. . . . They name and describe the one they call ineffable and unnameable, and just as if they had been attending physicians they tell about his emission and his generation, assimilating him to the Logos [word] emitted by mankind.

Theophilus had located the innate Logos in God's *splanchna,* but the inelegant metaphor did not appeal to Irenaeus. He ridiculed the notion that the Gnostic aeons were within the Father's viscera and insisted that nobody knew how the Son was produced (2.13.6; 28.6). Similarly Origen pointedly denied that Psalm 45:1 (see p. 75) refers to the Son.[20] Irenaeus referred later verses of the psalm to Christ "in his kingdom" but said nothing about verse 1 (4.33.11).

In addition, he rejected the distinction between the *Logos endiathetos* and the *Logos prophorikos* which Theophilus had applied to the divine Word. He addressed Gnostics as well, claiming that God, who is wholly Mind and wholly Logos, says what he thinks and thinks what he says; for God's Thought is God's Word, and the Word is Mind, and the all-enclosing Mind is the Father himself. No one knows the mode of the Son's generation (2.28.3–4). When Irenaeus rejects speculation about the generation of the Logos from the Father, he is sharply disagreeing with Theophilus as well as the Gnostics.

There is an interesting parallel between the two theologians. Theophilus apparently relied on the Jewish Targum to Genesis when he insisted that Logos and Sophia were creative powers, while Irenaeus learned from Jewish Christian exegetes that Genesis 1:1, *bereshith bara Elohim*, means "A Son in the beginning God established." He or his informant must have mistaken *bara* for a form of *bar*, son. The information was quite wrong, but it seemed useful for a more Son-centered Christology.[21] Both theologians thus relied on Jewish or Jewish Christian sources, and Irenaeus tried to correct Theophilus by making better use of Hebrew sources.

The Logos Incarnate

The incarnation of the Logos is another matter. Indeed, it is the key doctrine of Irenaeus' system. Sometimes he speaks of it rather simply, saying that "God became man and the Lord himself saved us, himself giving us the sign of the Virgin" (3.21.1). More fully, "God's Logos is our Lord Jesus Christ, who in the last days became a man among men in order to join the end to the beginning, that is, man to God" (4.20.4). Sometimes he relies on New Testament language, reminding us that, for example, "John knows only one and the same Logos of God, who is the Only-Begotten and became incarnate for our salvation, Jesus Christ our Lord" (3.16.2). He claims to prove that "the Word existed in the beginning with God; through him all things were made, and he was always present with the human race." Most recently, "at a moment fixed by the Father, he was united with the work shaped by him and was made a man subject to passions" (3.18.1). The Father fixed the moment in the divine plan (*oikonomia*) for the salvation of humanity.

Irenaeus seems to believe that the miraculous conception explains it, though he does not say how. Interestingly enough, he uses the passage from which Theophilus had taken his mysterious allusion to "Power of the Most High" as an example of what the Ebionites are "unwilling to understand" when they reject the incarnation (Luke 1:35; 5.1.3). Ultimately Irenaeus does not explain how it took place. On this point he may simply reiterate the ideas of Ignatius of Antioch, who listed divine attributes and then insisted that "for us" Christ accepted limitations. He was invisible but for us became visible, cannot suffer but for us accepted suffering, in every way endured for us.[22] Thus Irenaeus uses the terms of Ephesians and Ignatius when he says that Christ "recapitulated man in himself, the invisible made visible, the incomprehensible made comprehensible, unable to suffer but suffering; the Word, man." The summary is based on Ignatius, but the idea of "recapitulation," as we shall see, is Irenaeus' own.[23] What Irenaeus is doing is insisting upon the divinity of the human Jesus. Some of his predecessors had failed to achieve such a synthesis.

There are many points, especially in regard to the Old Testament, on which Irenaeus agrees with Theophilus. Like Theophilus he speaks of Adam as an infant; in Eden neither Adam nor Eve had any understanding of procreation; both had to grow up before they could increase and multiply (3.22.4).[24] Like Theophilus (2.25–27) he strongly emphasizes Adam's free will and refers to deification and immortality as the result of obedience to God (*Heresies* 4.37–39). Like Theophilus (2.24), Irenaeus rejects the view of "certain persons"—presumably Marcionites—that God begrudged Adam the tree of life and claims that God expelled him from paradise out of pity (*Heresies* 3.23.6; Theophilus 2.26 speaks of mercy and patience). Irenaeus' statement that disobedience, not the law, results in punishment (5.26.2), however, is based not on Theophilus (2.25) but, as he says, on Justin. His basic source for teaching about Adam is Theophilus, however.

Irenaeus was not content simply to use Theophilus' thoughts. Sometimes he provides severe criticism, though without naming a fellow bishop. For example, the two authors disagree over the interpretation of Romans 5:10 and 19, for Theophilus treats Christ's work as exemplary while Irenaeus considers it efficacious. We have already seen how Theophilus distorts Paul (chapter 5). Here is another comparison of texts, to show how much closer Irenaeus is to Paul's thought.

To Autolycus 2.28	*Heresies* 3.18.7
As by disobedience man gained	As by disobedience of the one man who was first formed from the crude earth the many were made sinners and
death for himself,	lost life,
so by obedience to the will	so by obedience of the one man who was first born of a virgin the many were made righteous
of God whoever will can obtain eternal life for himself.	and obtain salvation.

Or again:

	Heresies 3.21.10
	As by disobedience of the one man brought forth the fruit of life for men formerly dead.

The contradiction is not absolute, but the emphases are quite different. Theophilus "dechristologizes" Romans; Irenaeus does not. Presumably he is correcting Theophilus in the light of his own more biblical, philosophical, and traditional theology.

The Life of Jesus

Irenaeus is deeply concerned with the reality of the human life of Jesus. It began with his birth by the Holy Spirit and the Virgin Mary, who was a descendant of David (3.21.5), at Bethlehem about the forty-first year of Augustus (3.20.4, 21.3). He was truly flesh and blood (5.14.1) and, indeed, was "in the likeness of sinful flesh" (3.20.2; Rom. 8:3). His flesh was subject to the ills and limitations of humanity (3.22.2, 5.21.2). He died as a man and rose in the flesh (5.7.1, 31.2). For most of these points Irenaeus obviously relied on the Synoptic Gospels and their implications, as well as selected texts from the Gospel of John. His "orthodox" picture of Christ was based on the documents now regarded as canonical—notably on Luke, whose Gospel provided uniquely valuable evidence (3.14.3).

In addition, he quotes many texts that report the teaching of Jesus, including several that had already been cited by the apologists Justin and Theophilus. Such texts dealt with the avoidance of lust (4.13.1, 16.5; Matt. 5:28) and the love of enemies (Matt. 5:44, 46).[25] Irenaeus notes that the incarnate Logos actually practiced love of enemies when he was on the cross and quotes Luke 23:34 to prove the point (3.18.5).

The Future Resurrection

When Irenaeus writes that after the resurrection humankind will truly be concerned with imperishability, will grow and become strong in the times of the kingdom, until they become capable of containing the glory of the Father (5.35.2), he is following Theophilus' treatment of Christ's infant growth as related to humanity in general, but he has set it at the end rather than the beginning. He speaks of humanity in general, not Adam or Jesus alone, when he says that God "fashioned man for growth and increase" (4.11.1). He also modifies Theophilus' moralism when he comments that "as he who had been made a living soul lost his life when he turned to the worse, so this same man returning to the better and receiving the life-giving Spirit will find life" (5.12.2).

Irenaeus mentions the verses from Luke to which Theophilus alluded in his remarks about resurrection, but instead of letting Moses and the prophets have the last word on the resurrection, he insists that the words of Moses are, in fact, the words of Christ (4.2.3). Like Theophilus he argues for resurrection from the creation of humanity in the first place (5.3.2), but for further proof goes on, as we should expect, not to analogies from nature but to Christ's miracles of healing (5.12.6–13.1). He has already discussed them when opposing the Gnostics, also insisting that in local churches Christians were raised from the dead. (Gnostics said resurrection was simply gnosis.) When he added that Christians raised from the dead "have remained with us for many years" (2.31.2, 2.32.4), he may well have relied on the apology of Quadratus, which made the same point,[26] but in any event he goes beyond Theophilus' reticence about resurrections.

What he says about life after death is fairly "down to earth" but not fully materialistic. He agrees with Theophilus (2.24) that Eden was a real place to the east, but he also locates it somewhere above "this world." Before the End the righteous will be transferred into it (5.5.1). Surprisingly, however, Irenaeus' view is more "spiritual" than that of Origen, who taught that during this period all the saints will go east for their advanced education.[27]

Speculative Theology

Irenaeus does not simply maintain the tradition handed down to him. We have already seen him introducing Xenophanes for his doctrine of God and using Theophilus' picture of Logos and Sophia as God's two hands. Now we should point out that in his Christology he also introduces some novel refinements. First, when he discusses the fall of Adam and its consequences, he carefully examines the language of Genesis 1:26: "after our Image and Likeness" and insists (most of the time) that humanity lost the Likeness but not the Image found in human flesh and apparently closely related to intelligence and free will (*Heresies* 4.38.4). This is an exegetical conclusion from the book of Genesis, where humankind in general is created not after the Likeness but after the Image,[28] and Adam begets "after his form [*eidea*] and after his Image" (5:3). He uses this subtle point, found in no Christian theologian before him,[29] to differentiate the Image, not lost in the Fall, from the Likeness, lost but restored by the Logos (5.16.2) and completed by the Spirit (5.6.1).[30]

Irenaeus also developed a theory about the divine plan effective in God's various covenants with his people. The terms "divine plan" (*oikonomia*) and "recapitulation" (*anakephalaiōsis*) come from the New Testament, specifically from the Pauline letters; indeed, both words occur in one mysterious and semi-Gnostic passage in Ephesians (1:9–10). God "has made known to us in all wisdom and insight the mystery of his will, according to his purpose which he set forth in Christ, as a plan [*oikonomia*] for the fulness of time, to unite [recapitulate, *anakephalaiōsasthai*] all things in him."

Before Irenaeus the Gnostics used the word "divine plan" of the emission of "Christ" and "Holy Spirit," as well as "Savior," so that the lost tranquillity of the aeons within the Pleroma would be restored.[31] Irenaeus' divine plan was quite different and involved the "recapitulation," or "reenactment,"[32] of human history in Christ. Valentinian Gnostics had already seized upon the mysterious verb "recapitulate" (Eph. 1:10) but laid emphasis on the "summing up" of "all" in the spiritual Christ (1.3.5). Irenaeus took the expression quite differently and held that "Christ reenacted all earlier events, leading them to their destination."[33] For him as for Paul "there is one God the Father and one Christ Jesus our Lord, who came through the whole divine plan [*oikonomia*] and recapitulated everything in himself. 'Everything' includes the man shaped by God; so he also recapitulated man in himself, from invisible becoming visible, from incomprehensible, comprehensible, from impassible, passible; from Logos, man" (3.16.6).[34] Adam was taken from the "virgin" earth and "just so, the Logos, reenacting Adam in himself, received from Mary, still a virgin, the generation which is the reenactment of Adam" (3.21.10).

Irenaeus takes the reenactment quite literally and, indeed, speculatively. Christ passed through all the stages of human development. "Even though he was perfect he became an infant like us, not for himself but because of the infancy of mankind" (4.38.2). This statement too may be modifying what Theophilus had said about Adam, and probably the Second Adam as well, who was not perfect at the beginning but became so by obedience. Unfortunately Irenaeus believed that Jesus came to save all age groups by passing through them: infancy, childhood (as a model of "piety, justice and submission," ideas taken from Luke), adolescence, young manhood, and advanced age. He held that "young manhood" extends until forty, when the decline toward old age sets in—or perhaps around fifty, in the light of "You are not yet fifty" in John 8:57 (2.22.4–6). He dated the birth of Jesus in the forty-second year of Augustus (3.21.3; presumably 3 B.C.), and naturally set his mission in the reign of Tiberius (4.22.2; Luke 3:1). But if he lived to be forty or fifty, the crucifixion had to take place under Caligula (37–41) or Claudius (41–54); and in his *Demonstration* 74 Irenaeus calls Pontius Pilate "the governor of Claudius Caesar." History has yielded to theory because Irenaeus is unduly concerned with his speculative point about ages.

He deals with another speculative point more adequately. This is the question of the relation between the human and the divine in the incarnate Christ.[35] Relying on the scriptures, he declares that Christ is

> man without beauty, subject to suffering, seated on the foal of an ass, given vinegar and gall to drink, despised by the people, descending even to death; on the other hand, holy Lord, wonderful Counselor, shining with beauty, the mighty God, coming on the clouds as Judge of all (3.19.2).

But these appellations do not finally explain the mystery of the passion. Irenaeus adds his own meditations:

First, "as he was man in order to be tempted, so he was also Logos in order to be glorified" [cf. John 1:14], and second, "on the one hand, the Logos remained quiescent when the Lord was tempted, dishonored, crucified and put to death; on the other, the man was 'swallowed up' [1 Cor. 15:53–54; 2 Cor. 5:4] when he was victorious and endured and showed mercy and arose and was assumed into heaven" (3.19.3).

Here, however, Irenaeus was relying on the human psychology he had already refused to use in speaking of God. He had said that "according to the Greeks, the Logos as the first principle which thinks is one thing and the organ by means of which the word is emitted is another; sometimes a man remains 'quiescent' and silent and sometimes he speaks and acts" (2.28.4); and Irenaeus went on to contrast human beings with God who is all Mind and all Logos. One would think he should not have referred to the "quiescence" of the divine Logos in the incarnate Christ.

Others had spoken of the silence of the Logos but at a point prior to the creation. Ignatius had referred to "the Logos that proceeded from silence";[36] and Marcellus of Ancyra was to arouse the ire of Eusebius by referring to the Logos within the silent God.[37]

Irenaeus' Own Conclusions

Irenaeus also set forth the main points of his work against heresies in a rather brief treatise or "manual of essentials" written for relatively advanced Christians (he mentions the earlier work in c. 99 of the manual). This *Epideixis* or *Demonstration of the Apostolic Preaching* is now extant only in Armenian, but the Greek original was mentioned by Eusebius. The phrase "apostolic preaching" does not occur in *Against Heresies*, but it is obviously the same as the "preaching of the apostles" on which Irenaeus insists.[38] In the last of these passages he cites 1 Corinthians 15:11, with its emphasis on the unity of the proclamation. Neither "demonstration" nor "apostolic preaching" occurs in the New Testament, and Irenaeus thus demonstrates his liberty in regard to the expressions of scripture as well as his devotion to the biblical narrative from creation through resurrection. Much of the "demonstration" consists of a retelling of the story in relation to Christ.

He begins with a very simple baptismal formula: "in the name of Jesus Christ, the Son of God, who was incarnate and died and rose again" (3). He then expands it as he states "the second heading of our faith": "the Logos of God, Son of God, Christ Jesus our Lord, who was manifested to the prophets . . . ; through whom all things were made; who also at the end of the times, to complete and sum up all things, was made man among men, visible and tangible, in order to abolish death and show forth life and produce a commonality between God and humanity" (6). He adds that "God is glorified forever by his Logos, who is his Son," and—still correcting Theophilus—differentiates Son from Holy Spirit and Logos from Sophia (10). From this point onward he retells the biblical story and sets forth his theory of recapitulation or reenactment before turning to Christ in prophecy and incarnation.

Proof that the Son existed before the world comes from the first two words of the Hebrew Genesis, which, as we have said, Irenaeus' ideas about Hebrew allow him to translate as "a Son in the beginning." More reliably, he quotes John 1:1–3, explains that the Logos "was in the beginning *with* the Father" (43), and goes on to claim that as the Father is Lord and the Son is Lord, so the Father is God and the Son is God, for what is begotten of God is God (47).

The Christ of the Second Century

Irenaeus marks the end of our study, though he lived long before the major Christological debates of Nicaea and Chalcedon. With his thought, however, a clearly definable process has come to an end. During the second century various Christians used the primary but preliminary New Testament portrayals of Jesus in relation to creation, redemption, history, and eschatology, and they made two basic mistakes. The first attempts along such lines were made by Gnostic teachers, ea-

ger to cling to the divine Christ by jettisoning Jesus' historical humanity. Their attempts were rejected by Christian
leaders throughout the Greco-Roman world, especially by
apologists who were developing doctrines of the Logos and by
Jewish Christians maintaining the humanity of Jesus. The
writings of Theophilus of Antioch exemplify an opposite ten-
dency. He developed the Logos doctrine in a way that took it
close to Greco-Roman philosophy and mythology at the same
time, while on the other hand he spoke about Jesus as
prophet, moral teacher, and restorer of the human good lost
by Adam. His picture of Logos cooperating with Sophia in the
work of creation led to a mythological scene that recalled
Philo's language about Logos and Sophia as son and daugh-
ter of God and paralleled Greek ideas about Zeus and Athena.
His Logos apparently did not become incarnate.

Irenaeus was opposed to both Gnosticism and apologetic
excess. He returned to the Bible and constantly quoted texts,
usually without allegorizing them, even though he was developing a theological system partly based on Greco-Roman philosophy and psychological teaching. He was able to produce a
picture of Christianity which, as F. C. Burkitt noted fifty
years ago,[39] tends to sound commonplace "chiefly because the
main lines of Christian theology and of Biblical interpretation followed the same course down to a hundred years ago"—
we should now have to say, "a hundred and fifty." Irenaeus
did not altogether avoid speculative theology, or try to do so
any more than the apostles did. His synthesis endured for
many centuries, however, and therefore deserves the sympa-
thetic attention of later theologians.

Appendix:
Irenaeus and the Process
of Thought

The Gnostic Basilides held a doctrine of emanations in which the "unborn Father" brought forth Logos, followed by Understanding (*phronēsis*), Wisdom (*sophia*), and Power (*dynamis*), then three kinds of angelic powers.[1] In order to oppose this scheme, Irenaeus relied on Middle Platonic analysis of the thought process (2.13.2).[2] Mind, he said, is the ruling element (*principale* = *hēgemonikon*), the first principle and source of all intellectual activity, and *ennoia* is a particular movement proceeding from it and related to a determinate object. Mind, "the father of thought," contains within itself the motions of the hidden and invisible thought process in accordance with which they continue and increase.[3]

> The first motion of the mind in relation to anything is called Notion [*ennoia*]. When it continues and grows and takes hold of the whole soul it is called *enthymēsis*. When *enthymēsis* remains the same for a long time and is tested [*probata*], it is called *sensatio*. *Sensatio* long continued and amplified becomes *consilium*. When *consilium* grows and amplifies it is called *cogitatio*, and as it perseveres in the mind it is most rightly [*rectissime*] called *verbum*, from which *emissibilis verbum* proceeds.[4]

Stoic or Middle Platonic

The language of this statement is Stoic at the beginning and the end, for it lays emphasis on *ennoia*, "notion," and differentiates *logos endiathetos*, "inner discourse" (perhaps with an allusion to the *orthos logos* as well), and *logos prophorikos*, the "expressed word." Well before Irenaeus, however, these terms had been appropriated by the Platonic schools; Albinus offers examples.[5] Orbe has tried to claim all the terms for Stoicism, but difficulty arises partly because the Latin version may not render the terms correctly and partly because the middle terms (*enthymēsis, sensatio, consilium,* and *cogitatio*) do not seem to be Stoic. By using the *Lexicon* of Reynders and the suggestions of Orbe, we may discover what they mean. *Enthymēsis* means "consideration" or "reflection," and Irenaeus' Latin version once translates it as *excogitatio* (1.3.4; cf. 2.18.4). It is reasonable to translate *sensatio* as *phronēsis* or forethought or even "planning"; and Orbe (368 n. 24) compares Clement, *Stromata* 6.154.4, where the definition is Platonic, not Stoic.[6] *Consilium* must be *boulēsis* or "deliberation," while *cogitatio* is *dialogismos* or "inner discourse."[7]

Platonic, but Not "Orthodox" Platonic

Unfortunately there seems to be no text, either Stoic or Platonic, in which these mental phases are named. A few chapters later Irenaeus himself abbreviates the list and mentions only Mind, Ennoia, Enthymesis, and two stages of Logos "according to the Greeks" (2.28.4). Presumably his Enthymesis is equivalent to all the middle terms he named earlier.

In any event, it is hard to pin philosophers of this period down to a special vocabulary. Such an "orthodox" Platonist as Atticus, head of the school at Athens in Irenaeus' time, spoke of the soul's primary motions as "deliberating, reflecting, conjecturing, remembering, and reasoning."[8] Plato himself had used different Greek words in referring to "willing, reflecting, thinking ahead, deliberating, and holding true and false opinions."[9]

Mental Growth or Divine Thought

After his discussion of the mental phases, Plato refers to the growth and continuity of the human body, analogous to that of the mind. It is first youthful, next mature, then old. "It receives these appellations as it develops and endures, not in relation to a change of substance or loss of the body" (2.13.2).[10] It may be significant that Stoics related physical age to mental phases that developed at ages seven and fourteen.[11] Obviously Irenaeus' analysis is incomplete, but his source may have gone further.

He passes from this discussion of human psychology to the differences between God's thinking and human thought. Scripture teaches that the thoughts of God are not like human thoughts (Isa. 55:8-9)—and so, we may add, does Xenophanes: "There is one god, greatest among gods and men, neither in form nor in thought resembling mortals."[12] Irenaeus then proceeds to paraphrase the familiar fragment of Xenophanes (21 B 24) thus: "God is wholly Mind, wholly Thought, wholly Reason, wholly Hearing, wholly Eye, wholly Light, and wholly Source of all good"(2.13.3).

This analysis suggests that in key passages of Irenaeus' ideas about rational thought he was relying on pagan models in which Stoic, pre-Socratic, and Platonic elements were present. In the Hellenistic age such a mixture could be found in Middle Platonism, whose founder Antiochus of Ascalon "accepted the Stoic doctrine of certainty, the doctrine of the *kataleptikē phantasia*, or . . . 'cognitive impression.' "[13]

It is not surprising, then, that one of the few good philosophical parallels to Irenaeus' picture of mental processes can be found in the *Lucullus* (30) of Cicero, in a passage based on Antiochus.

> The mind, which is the source of the sensations . . . , has a natural force which it directs to the things by which it is moved. Accordingly it seizes on some sense-presentations so as to make use of them at once, others it stores away, as it were . . . , while it unites all the rest into systems by their mutual resemblances, and from these are formed the concepts of objects which the Greeks sometimes call *ennoiai*, sometimes *prolepseis*. When reason and logical proof and an innumerable multi-

tude of facts have been added, then comes the clear perception of all these things.

This is not far from what Irenaeus said about thinking, but his Christological thought did not develop along these lines.

Notes

Preface

1. Eusebius *Church History* 6.12.1.

2. C. Cuttell, *Philip Carrington* (Toronto: Anglican Book Centre, 1988), 60.

Chapter 1. Biblical Christology: The Humanity of Christ

1. Cf. Isa. 7:13, 9:7, 11:1–10; Jer. 23:5–6; Micah 5:2; Zech. 9:9–10.

2. This notion is somehow modified in Mark 12:35–37, where Jesus explains that the Messiah is David's Lord, not his son.

3. Eusebius *Church History* 1.7.13–14. Was the village Kochaba related to the messianic claimant Bar Kochba—with an inferior genealogy?

4. Cf. *Clementine Homilies* 18.13.3.

5. Norman Perrin firmly, and I believe rightly, rejected the "authenticity" of this text.

6. Justin *Dialogue* 48.1.5 (cf. 49.1).

7. Cf. Mark 2:15–17 and parallels.

8. Justin *Apology* 1.23.2.

9. Origen *Commentary on Matthew* 13.26.

10. Judg. 14:19, 15:14, cf. 13:25.

11. Cf. Luke 9:19; Matt. 16:14; Mark 8:28.

12. Matt. 12:41–42; Luke 11:32; Matt. 12:6.

13. For Jesus as prophet in Luke cf. W. Schmeichel, "Soteriology in the Theology of Luke" (Ph.D. diss., University of Chicago, 1975), 188–235.

14. Cf. Justin *Dialogue* 31.1.

15. G. W. H. Lampe, *A Patristic Greek Lexicon* (Oxford: Clarendon Press, 1968), 1428a.

16. Ignatius *Ephesians* 20.2.

17. Justin *Dialogue* 76.1.

18. Irenaeus *Heresies* 5.21.1.

19. Ibid. 3.19.1.

20. Ibid. 1.30.1; others identified the Third Man as Adam and the Son of Man as Jesus born of Mary; cf. Hippolytus *Refutation* 5.6.4–7. R. Reitzenstein went so far as to ascribe both the Gnostic "Man" and the supposed Jewish "Son of Man" figure to Iranian speculation, but modern scholarship—well summarized by T. H. Tobin, *The Creation of Man: Philo and the History of Interpretation* (Washington, D.C.: Catholic Biblical Quarterly Monograph Series 14, 1983), 102–108—more reasonably views the speculation as either Manichaean, and therefore late, or originally Jewish and based on Genesis. Cf. G. Quispel, "Der gnostische Anthropos und die jüdische Tradition," *Eranos Jahrbuch* 22 (1953): 195–254; H.-M. Schenke, *Der Gott "Mensch" in der Gnosis* (Göttingen: Vandenhoeck & Ruprecht, 1962).

21. Clement *Excerpts* 61.4.

22. Summary by J. N. D. Kelly, *Early Christian Creeds* (London: Longmans, 1950), 11–12.

Chapter 2. Biblical Christology: The Divinity of Christ

1. On this point cf. L. L. Welborn, "Georgi's *Gegner*," *Journal of Religion* 68 (1988): 566–574.

2. I discussed them in "The Coming of the Kingdom," *Journal of Biblical Literature* 67 (1948): 300.

3. The feeding and resurrection miracles of Elijah and Elisha in the books of Kings were especially important.

4. S. G. Hall, *Melito of Sardis* On Pascha *and Fragments* (Oxford: Clarendon Press, 1979), 68–71, xxx–xxxi.

5. Philo *Laws of Allegory* 3.96.

6. I have already criticized the Corinthians passage in my 1974–75 Tuohy Lectures: J. F. Kelly, ed., *Perspectives on Scripture and Tradition* (Notre Dame, Ind.: Fides, 1976), 5–6.

7. F. Loofs, "Das altkirchliche Zeugnis gegen die herrschende Auffassung der Kenosisstelle (Phil 2.5 bis 11)," *Theologische Studien und Kritiken* 100 (1927/28): 1–10.

8. J. Gewiess, "Zum altkirchlichen Verständnis der Kenosisstelle (Phil 2,5–11)," *Theologische Quartalschrift* 128 (1948): 463–487.

9. Philo *On Creation* 71.

10. Cf. my *Gods and the One God* (Philadelphia: Westminster Press, 1986), 102–104, 120–121; cf. A. Henrichs, "The Sophists and Hellenistic Religion," *Harvard Studies in Classical Philology* 88 (1984): 154.

11. Philo *On the Cherubim* 125–127; J. Weiss, *Der erste Korintherbrief* (Göttingen: Vandenhoeck & Ruprecht, 1910), 222–227; my article, "Causation and the 'Ancient World-View,'" *Journal of Biblical Literature* 83 (1964): 34–40.

12. Cf. Weiss, *Der erste Korintherbrief,* 226.

13. Philo *Flight* 51.

14. Origen *Against Celsus* 5.41.

15. Weiss cites Wisdom of Solomon 9:1–2; Philo *Laws of Allegory* 1.55, etc.

16. J. Rendel Harris, *The Origins of the Prologue to St. John's Gospel* (Cambridge: Cambridge University Press, 1917).

17. R. Bultmann, *Das Evangelium des Johannes* (Göttingen: Vandenhoeck & Ruprecht, 1941), 8–10.

18. Ptolemaeus in Irenaeus *Heresies* 1.8.4.

19. Theophilus *To Autolycus* 2.22; from Theophilus, Irenaeus *Heresies* 3.8.3; Clement *Exhortation* 7.3; 110.1; *Tutor* 1.62.4.

20. Justin *Dialogue* 62.4; Irenaeus *Heresies* 3.18.1; cf. F. Loofs, *Theophilus von Antiochien und die anderen theologischen Quellen bei Irenaeus* (*Texte und Untersuchungen* 46.2, 1930), 55–56, 68–69, 350–351.

21. Tertullian *Against Praxeas* 21.2.

22. Epiphanius *Heresies* 65.1.5.

23. Marcellus Frag. 52 Klostermann.

24. Origen *Against Celsus* 2.31.

25. Bultmann, *Das Evangelium des Johannes,* 39.

26. Irenaeus *Heresies* 1.8.5.

27. M. Theobald, *Die Fleischwerdung des Logos: Studien zur Verhaltung des Johannesprologs zum Corpus des Evangeliums und zu 1 Joh;* Neutestamentliche Abhandlungen, Neue Folge, 20 (Münster: Aschendorff, 1988).

28. John 13:34; 1 John 3:11, etc.

29. Justin *Apology* 1.66.2.

30. Philo *Agriculture* 51; *Corpus Hermeticum* 1.5.

31. Arthur Darby Nock, *Essays on Religion and the Ancient World,* ed. Z. Stewart (Oxford: Clarendon Press, 1972), 2:931.

32. Suetonius *Domitian* 13.2; other references in G. W. Mooney, *C. Suetoni Tranquilli De Vita Caesarum Libri VII-VIII* (London: Longmans, 1930), 570–572.

33. Clement *Stromata* 6.39.3.

34. Cf. Luke 24:39; Ignatius *Smyrnaeans* 3.2.

35. *Polycarp* 3.2; cf. W. R. Schoedel, *Ignatius of Antioch* (Philadelphia: Fortress Press, 1985), 267.

Chapter 3. Gnostic Christologies

1. Justin *Apology* 1.26.3, 8.

2. On Helen's desire to return cf. *Exegesis on the Soul* in J. M. Robinson, *The Nag Hammadi Library,* 2nd ed. (San Francisco: Harper & Row, 1988), 197–198.

3. Homer *Iliad* 2.177–178 (cf. 3.156–160); Herodotus 1.4.2; Plutarch *Herodotus* 856F; Hermogenes *Method* 32 (pp. 448–449 Rabe); Athenaeus 560B; Horace *Satires* 1.3.107–108; *Priapea* 68.

4. Irenaeus *Heresies* 1.23.1.

5. Ibid. 1.23.2–3.

6. Ibid. 1.24.1.

7. Eusebius *Chronicle* p. 201 Helm.

8. Justin *Apology* 1.31.6; cf. J. T. Milik, "Une lettre de Siméon bar Kokhba," *Revue Biblique* 60 (1953): 276–294; Aristo in Eusebius *Church History* 4.2.6.

9. Irenaeus *Heresies* 1.24.3; see Appendix: "Irenaeus and the Process of Thought."

10. Ibid. 1.20.25.

11. A. Harnack, *Marcion. Das Evangelium vom fremden Gott* (2nd ed., Leipzig: Hinrichs, 1924), 291*, 293*; Tertullian *Against Marcion* 3.21, 3.24.1, 4.33.8.

12. Harnack, *Marcion,* 229; 124–126.

13. Clement *Excerpts from Theodotus* 60; Hippolytus *Refutation* 6.35.3–4.

14. Irenaeus *Heresies* 1.15.3.

15. Ibid. 1.8.4.

16. Clement *Excerpts from Theodotus* 61.2.

17. Ibid. 61.

18. Origen made a similar point out of Johannine texts: cf. *Commentary on John* 19.2; *Against Celsus* 7.16; cf. H. Chadwick, "Ori-

gen, Celsus, and the Stoa," *Harvard Theological Review* 41 (1948): 100 n. 30.

19. Clement *Excerpts from Theodotus* 66.

20. Again Origen speaks similarly in the *Commentary on Matthew* 12.16–17; cf. M. Harl, *Origène et la fonction révélatrice du Verbe incarné* (Paris: du Seuil, 1958), 260.

21. Cf. Harnack, *Marcion,* 256*–259*.

22. Irenaeus *Heresies* 1.25.

23. M. Smith, *Clement of Alexandria and a Secret Gospel of Mark* (Cambridge, Mass.: Harvard University Press, 1973), I.23–II.2.

Chapter 4. Christology in the Apostolic Fathers and Justin

1. *1 Clem.* 59.2.4.

2. Cf. J. T. Lienhard, "The Christology of the Epistle to Diognetus," *Vigiliae Christianae* 24 (1970): 280–289.

3. A. C. Sundberg, Jr., "Canon Muratori: A Fourth-Century List," *Harvard Theological Review* 66 (1973): 1–41; confirmed by G. M. Hahneman (D.Phil. diss., Oxford University, 1987).

4. J. N. D. Kelly, *Early Christian Creeds* (London: Longmans, 1950), 68–69; Trall. 9.

5. Cf. 1 John 4:2–3; 2 John 7.

6. Irenaeus *Heresies* 3.3.4.

7. Epiphanius *Panarion* 33.3.9.

8. Irenaeus *Heresies* 1.25.6.

9. Kelly, *Early Christian Creeds,* 73.

10. Justin *Dialogue with Trypho* 41.1.

11. Kelly, *Early Christian Creeds,* 73–75.

12. Theophilus will be more evasive: Christians are so called because anointed with the oil of God.

13. Justin *Apology* 1.21.1.

14. Ibid. 22–23. Perseus, Asclepius, and Dionysus, though not the Logos Hermes, recur in *Dialogue* 67–70.

15. Justin *Dialogue* 61.1, 3, 62.4, 100.4, 126.1.

16. Numenius Frag. 14 = Eusebius *Preparation for the Gospel* 11.18.16.

17. H. von Arnim, *Stoicorum Veterum Fragmenta* III 141; II 739 = Origen *Against Celsus* 1.37.

18. Ibid. II 1074 = Origen *Against Celsus* 4.48, cf. 580.

19. Seneca *Epistle* 12.11, 16.7.

20. Clement *Stromata* 1.37.6.

21. Details in A. J. Droge, "Justin Martyr and the Restoration of Philosophy," *Church History* 56 (1987): 303–319, esp. 313–314.

22. For Paul cf. O. Skarsaune, *The Proof from Prophecy,* Supplements to Novum Testamentum, 66 (Leiden: Brill, 1987), 92–100.

23. For the Christian "second God" cf. the beginning of Origen's *Dialogue with Heraclides;* also *Against Celsus* 5.39, 6.61.

24. Numenius Frag. 21 = Proclus *Commentary on the Timaeus* i.303 Diehl; Frag. 11 = Eusebius *Preparation for the Gospel* 11.18.3.

25. J. N. D. Kelly, *Early Christian Doctrines* (New York: Harper & Brothers, 1958), 103.

26. Luke 1:15, 35, 41, 67, 2:25–26.

27. He thus echoes both parts of Luke 1:35, and quotes them in *Dialogue* 100.5.

28. John 1:14, 18; Justin *Dialogue* 105.1, 128.3.

29. 1 Cor. 8:6; John 1:3.

Chapter 5. The Jewish Christian Christology of Theophilus

1. Eusebius *Church History* 5.28.5.

2. Hippolytus *Refutation* 7.35; cf. 10.23.

3. They thus accepted Irenaeus' claim that Roman doctrine was apostolic and normative—up to his time.

4. Eusebius *Church History* 5.28.3–6.

5. Hippolytus *Refutation* 9.11.3.

6. Eusebius *Church History* 5.28.11–12.

7. J. Armitage Robinson, *St. Irenaeus: The Apostolic Preaching* (London: SPCK, 1920), 54.

8. J. Bentivegna, "A Christianity Without Christ," *Texte und Untersuchungen* 116 (1975): 107–130, esp. 128–130.

9. Samuel Laeuchli, *The Language of Faith* (New York: Abingdon Press, 1962), 165.

10. Luke 4:18 with Acts 10:38; M. de Jonge, *Christology in Context* (Philadelphia: Westminster Press, 1988), 100; Justin *Apology* 2.6.3.

11. Cf. also Hippolytus *Refutation* 5.9.22.

12. A. Harnack, *Marcion. Das Evangelium vom fremden Gott* (*Texte und Untersuchungen* 45, 1924), 421*–23*.

13. E. R. Goodenough, *Introduction to Philo Judaeus* (New Haven: Yale University Press, 1940), 43–44.

14. Most recently and reliably, D. A. Fiensy, *Prayers Alleged to Be Jewish,* Brown Judaic Studies, 65 (Chico, Calif.: Scholars Press,

1985), 138–140; for Theophilus cf. "The Early Antiochene Anaphora," *Anglican Theological Review* 30 (1940): 91–94.

15. H. J. Schoeps, *Theologie und Geschichte des Judenchristentums* (Tübingen: Mohr, 1949), 174–175; A. Marmorstein, *Studies in Jewish Theology* (London: Oxford University Press, 1950), 1–71; *Clementine Homilies* 2.43–44.

16. Philo *Allegory of the Laws* 1.65.

17. *Targum du Pentateuque,* trans. R. Le Déaut (Paris: Cerf, 1976), I. 74 (*Sources Chrétiennes* 245).

18. Tertullian *Against Hermogenes* 18.6; cf. *Against Praxeas* 7.1; *Against Marcion* 2.4.1.

19. *1 Clement* 2.1, 23.1; Ignatius *Philadelphians* 10.1.

20. A. S. Pease, *M. Tullii Ciceronis De Natura Deorum* (Cambridge, Mass.: Harvard University Press, 1955), 1:276.

21. Hesiod *Theogony* 886–890, 900, 924–926, 929 a–f; S. Kauer, *Die Geburt der Athena im altgriechischen Epos* (Würzburg: Triltsch, 1959), 11.14.

22. *nēdyn: Theogony* 886, 888, 890, 899, and 929h.

23. C. Curry, "The Theogony of Theophilus," *Vigiliae Christianae* 42 (1988): 318–326.

24. D. A. Russell and N. G. Wilson, *Menander Rhetor* (Oxford: Clarendon Press, 1981), 22–23.

25. *Stoicorum Veterum Fragmenta* II 908–909, cf. 894.

26. Pseudo-Dionysius *Oration* 7, vol. 6, p. 285 Radermacher.

27. Origen *Against Celsus* 8.67.

28. In *Oration* 43.9 Aristides calls Zeus "the Beginning of all."

29. Justin *Dialogue* 62.4 refers to Proverbs for this "conversation."

30. *Stoicorum Veterum Fragmenta* II 894.

31. Cf. M. Muehl, "Der Logos endiathetos und prophorikos in der älteren Stoa bis zur Synode von Sirmium," *Archiv für Begriffsgeschichte* 7 (1962): 7–56.

32. Irenaeus *Heresies* 2.12.5, 13.6.8.

33. Origen *Against Celsus* 6.65.

34. M. Wiles, "Person or Personification? A Patristic Debate About Logos," in *The Glory of Christ in the New Testament,* ed. L. D. Hurst and N. T. Wright (Oxford: Clarendon Press, 1987), 281–289.

35. Philo *Posterity of Cain* 1–7.

36. Irenaeus *Heresies* 4.20.9–11, 28.1.

37. Clement *Pedagogue* 1.57.2; *Stromata* 5.34.1, 7.58.3; *Excerpts from Theodotus* 10.6, 12.1, 23.5.

38. Eusebius *Church History* 4.22.3.

39. Cf. G. W. Clarke, *The Octavius of Marcus Minucius Felix* (New York: Newman Press, 1974), 30.

40. Hippolytus *Refutation* 10.23.1; Epiphanius *Panarion* 54.3.5.

41. Judg. 13:24; 1 Sam. 2:21, 26, 30:6.

42. Josephus *Antiquities* 2.230–231, 8.49; *Life* 8.

43. Cf. W. Dittenberger, *Sylloge Inscriptionum Graecarum,* 3rd ed., 708.18.

44. Cf. Origen *Commentary on Matthew* 13.26.

45. Cf. Schoeps, *Theologie und Geschichte des Judenchristentums,* 100–106.

46. Nemesius *Nature of Man* 5.

47. Theophilus *To Autolycus* 1.3, 11, 14 (Rom. 2:7); cf. 2.34.

48. Ibid. 2.8, 37; 3.9, 12.

49. Ibid. 2.10, 28, 30, 35, 38, 3.13.

50. Cf. W. Schmeichel, "Soteriology in the Theology of Luke" (Ph.D. diss., University of Chicago, 1975), 236–280.

51. Irenaeus *Heresies* 3.21.10; chapter 7.

52. W. Telfer, *Cyril of Jerusalem and Nemesius of Emesa* (Philadelphia: Westminster Press, 1955), 239 and note 4.

53. F. R. M. Hitchcock, "Loofs' Theory of Theophilus of Antioch as a Source of Irenaeus," *Journal of Theological Studies* 38 (1937): 265.

54. Cf. Theophilus *To Autolycus* 2.26, 3.9.

55. Eusebius *Church History* 6.17, on Symmachus.

56. Ibid. 3.27.

57. Eusebius *Church Theology* 1.20.43.

58. Eusebius *Church History* 6.12.3.

59. Cf. my "Conflict in Christology at Antioch," *Studia Patristica* 18 (1983): 1.140–151; and *Gods and the One God* (Philadelphia: Westminster Press, 1986), 133–134.

Chapter 6. Heresy and Christology

1. Eusebius *Church History* 5.20.1, 6.12.

2. Irenaeus *Heresies* 3.3.4.

3. Ibid. 4.6.2; cf. 5.26.2.

4. Eusebius *Church History* 4.23.4; cf. 4.25.

5. A. Le Boulluec, *La notion d'hérésie dans la littérature grecque*

IIe–IIIe siècles, vol. 1, *De Justin à Irénée* (Paris: Études Augustiniennes, 1985).

6. Ibid. 110.

7. Ibid. 90.

8. Ibid. 180.

9. W. Bauer, *Orthodoxy and Heresy in Earliest Christianity* (Philadelphia: Fortress Press, 1971), 103–104.

10. Irenaeus *Heresies* 3.3.3; cf. Le Boulluec, *La notion d'hérésie,* 21–22.

11. Irenaeus *Heresies* 3.4.3.

12. Ibid. 3.3.4.

13. Tertullian *Against Praxeas* 1.4–5.

14. Hippolytus *Refutation* 9.7.1, 11.1.3.

15. Justin *Dialogue* 80.5.

16. Ibid. 81.4.

17. Bauer, *Orthodoxy and Heresy,* 127.

18. Cf. Dionysius of Corinth in Eusebius *Church History* 4.23.9–11.

19. Eusebius *Church History* 6.36.4.

20. Irenaeus *Heresies* 3.3.3.

21. I repeat some points from my Walter and Mary Tuohy Lectures of 1974–75, published in *Perspectives on Scripture and Tradition,* ed. by J. F. Kelly (Notre Dame, Ind.: Fides, 1976), 33–34; cf. also L. Koep, "Consensus," *Reallexikon für Antike und Christentum* 3 (1957): 294–303, see esp. 296.

22. Cicero *Tusculan Disputations* 1.36.

23. Ibid. 1.39.

24. Aristotle *Rhetoric* 2.23.12, 1398b20–22.

25. Ibid. 1398b24–25.

26. Irenaeus *Heresies* 3.11.8.

27. Theophilus *To Autolycus* 1.1; also in Hermas *Vision* 3.6.6–7: *euchrēstos-achrēstos.*

28. A. Rousseau and L. Doutreleau, *Irénée de Lyon: Contre les hérésies Livre I* (Paris: Cerf, 1979), 1:31–35.

29. Irenaeus *Heresies* 5.15.3, 5.14.1, 1.16.3, 3.3.3–4.

30. Cf. Photius *Library* 232.

31. Eusebius *Church History* 5.26.

32. See my "The Apostolic Fathers' First Thousand Years," *Church History* 31 (1962): 421–429 = 57 Supplement (1988): 20–29.

33. C. Eggenberger, *Die Quellen der politischen Ethik des 1. Klemensbriefes* (Zurich: Zwingli-Verlag, 1951), 10–18.

34. Tatian *Oration* 35.

35. See F. Loofs, *Theophilus von Antiochien* (*Texte und Unter-suchungen* 46.2, 1930), 10–44 and 67–70; a few more examples are noted below.

36. See G. Kretschmar, *Studien zur frühchristlichen Trinitätstheologie* (Tübingen: Mohr, 1956), 33–42.

37. See W. R. Schoedel, "Enclosing, Not Enclosed," *Early Christian Literature and the Classical Intellectual Tradition*, ed. W. R. Schoedel and R. L. Wilken (Paris: Beauchesne, 1979), 75–86.

38. Irenaeus *Heresies* 3.3.2.

39. Eusebius *Church History* 5.24.11–17.

40. Ibid. 5.28.3–6.

Chapter 7. Irenaeus' Theology and Christology

1. See Robert M. Grant, "Place de Basilide dans la théologie chrétienne ancienne," trans. M. Simon, *Revue des Études Augustiniennes* 25 (1979): 201–216.

2. See W. Jaeger, *The Theology of the Early Greek Philosophers* (Oxford: Clarendon Press, 1947), 51–54, 212 n. 34.

3. See H. Diels and W. Kranz, *Die Fragmente der Vorsokratiker* 21 A 26.

4. Ibid. 21 B 24 = Sextus Empiricus *Against Professors* 9.144.

5. Ibid. 21 B 25, from Simplicius.

6. Ibid. 21 B 11 = Sextus Empiricus *Against Professors* 9.193.

7. Plato *Republic* 2.380C, 382E, 383A; solutions in Aristotle *Poetica* 1461a22; Proclus discussed by F. Buffière, *Les mythes d'Homère et la pensée grecque* (Paris: Belles Lettres, 1956), 554–555.

8. To Xenophanes' Mind, Eye, and Hearing, an intermediary has added Thought, Will, Light (cf. 1 John 1:5); Philo *Dreams* 1.75; the Savior as Mind and Light, *To Diognetus* 9.6.

9. Irenaeus *Heresies* 1.12.2, 2.13.3, 4.11.2; not in the repetitious 2.13.8 and 2.28.4.

10. Philo *Every Good Man Is Free* 84; Numenius Frag. 52 des Places = Calcidius 296.

11. Dionysius in Athanasius *Opinions of Dionysius* 23.2; Eusebius *Church Theology* 2.7.

12. M. Richard, "Un faux dithélite—Le traité de S. Irénée au Diacre Démétrius," *Polychronion: Festschrift Franz Doelger zum 75. Geburtstag*, ed. P. Wirth (Heidelberg: Winter, 1966), 431–440.

13. Clement *Stromata* 7.5.6; of God 7.37.4.

14. Irenaeus *Heresies* 1.22.1, 3.8.3; *Demonstration* 5.

15. Irenaeus *Heresies* Book 4 preface 4, 4.20.1, 5.1.3, 5.5.1, 5.6.1, 5.28.4; *Demonstration* 11.

16. See J. Mambrino, " 'Les Deux Mains de Dieu' dans l'oeuvre de saint Irénée," *Nouvelle Revue Théologique* 79 (1957): 355–370; one hand is Logos, 3.21.10.

17. Marcellus Frags. 59–60 Klostermann.

18. Methodius *Resurrection* 1.46.2; *Created Things* 9; Procopius on Gen. 1:27 in Migne, *Patrologia Graeca* 87.133A.

19. Irenaeus *Heresies* 2.28.5–6.

20. Origen *Commentary on John* 1.24, p. 29, 23 Preuschen; cf. R. Cadiou, *Commentaires inédits des Psaumes* (Paris: Belles Lettres, 1936), 77.

21. J. P. Smith, *St. Irenaeus: Proof of the Apostolic Preaching* (New York: Newman Press, 1952), 75; Irenaeus *Demonstration* 43.

22. Ignatius *To Polycarp* 3.2.

23. Irenaeus *Heresies* 3.16.6; cf. A. Houssiau, *La christologie de saint Irénée* (Louvain: Publications Universitaires, 1955), 231–232.

24. See G. Ruiz, "L'enfance d'Adam selon saint Irénée," *Bulletin de Littérature Ecclésiastique* 89 (1988): 97–111.

25. Justin *Apology* 1.15.1, 9; Theophilus *To Autolycus* 3.13–14.

26. Eusebius *Church History* 4.3.2.

27. Origen *First Principles* 2.11.6.

28. Gen. 1:27, 5:1, 9:6.

29. Philo thought that "likeness" simply made "image" more precise, *On the Creation* 71.

30. See N. P. Williams, *The Ideas of the Fall and of Original Sin* (London: Longmans, 1927), 194.

31. Irenaeus *Heresies* 1.7.2, 2.4–5, 6.1; cf. J. T. Nielsen, *Adam and Christ in the Theology of Irenaeus of Lyons* (Assen: Van Gorcum, 1968), 59.

32. J. Knudsen in G. T. Armstrong, *Die Genesis in der alten Kirche* (Tübingen: Mohr, 1962), 66.

33. Nielsen, *Adam and Christ* 66.

34. This language echoes and modifies Ignatius *Ephesians* 7.2.

35. On the text see Houssiau, *La christologie de saint Irénée*, 191–195; A. Rousseau and L. Doutreleau, *Irénée de Lyon: Contre les hérésies Livre III Tome I (Sources Chrétiennes* 210; Paris, 1974), 343–345.

36. Ignatius *Magnesians* 8.2; cf. W. R. Schoedel, *Ignatius of Antioch* (Philadelphia: Fortress Press, 1985), 120–122.

37. Eusebius *Against Marcellus* 1.1.4.

38. Irenaeus *Heresies* 1.10.1–2, 2.35.4, 3.3.3, 12.7, 13.1, 4.36.8, 5.13.4.

39. F. C. Burkitt, "Pagan Philosophy and the Christian Church," in *Cambridge Ancient History,* vol. 12 (Cambridge: Cambridge University Press, 1939), 475.

Appendix. Irenaeus and the Process of Thought

1. Irenaeus *Heresies* 1.23.3; cf. 1 Cor. 1:24; Col. 1:16.

2. A. Rousseau and L. Doutreleau, *Irénée de Lyon: Contre les hérésies Livre II* (Paris: Cerf, 1982), 1:236–240, 366–370; 2:110–115; see also E. P. Meijering, *God Being History* (Amsterdam: Elsevier/North Holland, 1975), 21–22.

3. A. Orbe, *Hacia la primera teología de la procesión del Verbo,* Estudios Valentinianos, 1/1, Analecta Gregoriana, 99 (Rome: Gregoriana, 1958), 363–386. ("Excursus: Las actividades mentales en la procesión del Logos.")

4. See "nourished and increased" and "impression in the soil," Sextus Empiricus *Against Professors* 7.233, 240.

5. Albinus *Eisagoge* 2; *Didaskalikos* p. 156, 17–18.

6. See S. R. C. Lilla, *Clement of Alexandria* (Oxford: Oxford University Press, 1971), 72–74.

7. Cf. Orbe, *Hacia la primera teología de la procesión del Verbo,* 368–371.

8. Atticus Frag. 7 Des Places = Eusebius *Preparation* 15.9.8.

9. Plato *Laws* 10.896E.

10. See the discussion of ages in Philo *Creation* 103–105; Irenaeus too believes in five ages, *Heresies* 2.22.4–6, 24.4.

11. *Stoicorum Veterum Fragmenta* II 834–835.

12. Diels-Kranz 21 B 23 = Clement of Alexandria *Stromata* 5.109.1.

13. J. Dillon, *The Middle Platonists* (London: Gerald Duckworth, 1977), 64.

Books and Articles Cited

Armstrong, G. T. *Die Genesis in der alten Kirche*. Tübingen: Mohr, 1962.

Bauer, W. *Orthodoxy and Heresy in Earliest Christianity*. Philadelphia: Fortress Press, 1971.

Bentivegna, J. "A Christianity Without Christ." *Texte und Untersuchungen* 116 (1975):107–130.

Buffière, F. *Les mythes d'Homère et la pensée grecque*. Paris: Belles Lettres, 1956.

Bultmann, R. *Das Evangelium des Johannes*. Göttingen: Vandenhoeck & Ruprecht, 1941.

Cadiou, R. *Commentaires inédits des Psaumes*. Paris: Belles Lettres, 1936.

Chadwick, H. "Origen, Celsus, and the Stoa." *Harvard Theological Review* 41 (1948): 100.

Clarke, G. W. *The Octavius of Marcus Minucius Felix*. New York: Newman Press, 1974.

Curry, C. "The Theogony of Theophilus." *Vigiliae Christianae* 42 (1988): 318–326.

Dillon, J. *The Middle Platonists*. London: Gerald Duckworth, 1977.

Droge, A. J. "Justin Martyr and the Restoration of Philosophy." *Church History* 56 (1987): 303–319.

Eggenberger, C. *Die Quellen der politischen Ethik des 1. Klemensbriefes*. Zurich: Zwingli Verlag, 1951.

Fiensy, D. A. *Prayers Alleged to Be Jewish*. Brown Judaic Studies 65. Chico, Calif.: Scholars Press, 1985.

Gewiess, J. "Zum altkirchlichen Verständnis der Kenosisstelle (Phil 2,5–11)." *Theologische Quartalschrift* 128 (1948): 463–487.

Goodenough, E. R. *Introduction to Philo Judaeus.* New Haven: Yale University Press, 1940.

Grant, R. M. "The Apostolic Fathers' First Thousand Years." *Church History* 31 (1962): 421–429 = 57 Supplement (1988): 20–29.

————. "Causation and the 'Ancient World-View.' " *Journal of Biblical Literature* 83 (1964): 34–40.

————. "The Coming of the Kingdom." *Journal of Biblical Literature* 67 (1948): 297–303.

————. "Conflict in Christology at Antioch." *Studia Patristica* 18 (1983): 1.140–151.

————. *Gods and the One God.* Philadelphia: Westminster Press, 1986.

————. "Place de Basilide dans la théologie chrétienne ancienne." Trans. M. Simon. *Revue des Études Augustiniennes* 25 (1979): 201–216.

Hall, S. G., ed. *Melito of Sardis*: On Pascha *and Fragments.* Oxford: Clarendon Press, 1979.

Harl, M. *Origène et la fonction révélatrice du Verbe incarné.* Paris: du Seuil, 1958.

Harnack, A. *Marcion. Das Evangelium vom fremden Gott.* 2nd ed. Leipzig: Hinrichs, 1924.

Harris, J. R. *The Origins of the Prologue to St. John's Gospel.* Cambridge: Cambridge University Press, 1917.

Henrichs, A. "The Sophists and Hellenistic Religion." *Harvard Studies in Classical Philology* 88 (1984): 139–158.

Hitchcock, F. R. M. "Loofs' Theory of Theophilus of Antioch as a Source of Irenaeus." *Journal of Theological Studies* 38 (1937): 265.

Houssiau, A. *La christologie de saint Irénée.* Louvain: Publications Universitaires, 1955.

Jaeger, W. *The Theology of the Early Greek Philosophers.* Oxford: Clarendon Press, 1947.

Jonge, M. de. *Christology in Context.* Philadelphia: Westminster Press, 1988.

Kauer, S. *Die Geburt der Athena im altgriechischen Epos.* Würzburg: Triltsch, 1959.

Kelly, J. F., ed. *Perspectives on Scripture and Tradition.* Notre Dame, Ind.: Fides, 1976.

Kelly, J. N. D. *Early Christian Creeds.* London: Longmans, 1950.

_____. *Early Christian Doctrines.* New York: Harper & Brothers, 1958.

Koep, L. "Consensus." *Reallexikon für Antike und Christentum* 3 (1957): 294–303.

Kretschmar, G. *Studien zur frühchristlichen Trinitätstheologie.* Tübingen: Mohr, 1956.

Laeuchli, S. *The Language of Faith.* New York: Abingdon Press, 1962.

Lampe, G. W. H. *A Patristic Greek Lexicon.* Oxford: Clarendon Press, 1968.

Le Boulluec, A. *La notion d'hérésie dans la littérature grecque IIe-IIIe siècles.* 2 vols. Paris: Études Augustiniennes, 1985.

Le Déaut, R., trans. *Targum du Pentateuque.* Paris: Cerf, 1976.

Lienhard, J. T. "The Christology of the Epistle to Diognetus." *Vigiliae Christianae* 24 (1970): 280–289.

Lilla, S. R. C. *Clement of Alexandria.* Oxford: Oxford University Press, 1971.

Loofs, F. "Das altkirchliche Zeugnis gegen die herrschende Auffassung der Kenosisstelle (Phil 2,5 bis 11)." *Theologische Studien und Kritiken* 100 (1927/28): 1–10.

_____. *Theophilus von Antiochien und die anderen theologischen Quellen bei Irenaeus. Texte und Untersuchungen* 46.2, 1930.

Mambrino, J. " 'Les Deux Mains de Dieu' dans l'oeuvre de saint Irénée." *Nouvelle Revue Théologique* 79 (1957): 355–370.

Marmorstein, A. *Studies in Jewish Theology.* London: Oxford University Press, 1950.

Meijering, E. P. *God Being History.* Amsterdam: Elsevier/North Holland, 1975.

Milik, J. T. "Une lettre de Siméon bar Kokhba." *Revue Biblique* 60 (1953): 276–294.

Mooney, G. W. *C. Suetoni Tranquilli De Vita Caesarum Libri VII-VIII.* London: Longmans, 1930.

Muehl, M. "Der Logos endiathetos und prophorikos in der älteren Stoa bis zur Synode von Sirmium." *Archiv für Begriffsgeschichte* 7 (1962): 7–56.

Nielsen, J. T. *Adam and Christ in the Theology of Irenaeus of Lyons.* Assen: Van Gorcum, 1968.

Nock, A. D. *Essays on Religion and the Ancient World.* 2 vols. Ed. Z. Stewart. Oxford: Clarendon Press, 1972.

Orbe, A. *Hacia la primera teología de la procesión del Verbo.* Estudios Valentinianos 1/1, Analecta Gregoriana 99. Rome: Gregoriana, 1958.

Pease, A. S. *M. Tullii Ciceronis De Natura Deorum.* 2 vols. Cambridge, Mass.: Harvard University Press, 1955.

Quispel, G. "Der gnostische Anthropos und die jüdische Tradition." *Eranos Jahrbuch* 22 (1953): 195–254.

Richard, M. "Un faux dithélite—Le traité de S. Irénée au Diacre Démétrius." *Polychronion: Festschrift Franz Doelger zum 75 Geburtstag.* Ed. P. Wirth. Heidelberg: Winter, 1966, 431–440.

Robinson, J. A. *St. Irenaeus: The Apostolic Preaching.* London: SPCK, 1920.

Robinson, J. M. *The Nag Hammadi Library.* San Francisco: Harper & Row, 1977.

Rousseau, A., and L. Doutreleau. *Irénée de Lyon: Contre les hérésies.* Paris: Cerf, *Livre I,* 1979; *Livre II,* 1982; *Livre III,* 1974.

Ruiz, G. "L'enfance d'Adam selon saint Irénée." *Bulletin de Littérature Ecclésiastique* 89 (1988): 97–111.

Russell, D. A., and N. G. Wilson. *Menander Rhetor.* Oxford: Clarendon Press, 1981.

Schenke, H.-M. *Der Gott "Mensch" in der Gnosis.* Göttingen: Vandenhoeck & Ruprecht, 1962.

Schmeichel, W. *Soteriology in the Theology of Luke.* Ph.D. diss., University of Chicago, 1975.

Schoedel, W. R. "Enclosing, Not Enclosed." In W. R. Schoedel and R. L. Wilken, eds., *Early Christian Literature* (see below), 75–86.

———. *Ignatius of Antioch.* Philadelphia: Fortress Press, 1985.

———, and R. L. Wilken, eds., *Early Christian Literature and the Classical Intellectual Tradition: in honorem Robert M. Grant.* Théologie Historique 54. Paris: Beauchesne, 1979.

Schoeps, H. J. *Theologie und Geschichte des Judenchristentums.* Tübingen: Mohr, 1949.

Skarsaune, O. *The Proof from Prophecy.* Supplements to Novum Testamentum, 66. Leiden: Brill, 1987.

Smith, J. P. *St. Irenaeus: Proof of the Apostolic Preaching.* New York: Newman Press, 1952.

Smith, M. *Clement of Alexandria and a Secret Gospel of Mark.* Cambridge, Mass.: Harvard University Press, 1973.

Sundberg, A. C., Jr. "Canon Muratori: A Fourth-Century List." *Harvard Theological Review* 66 (1973): 1–41.

Telfer, W. *Cyril of Jerusalem and Nemesius of Emesa.* Philadelphia: Westminster Press, 1955.

Theobald, M. *Die Fleischwerdung des Logos: Studien zur Verhaltung des Johannesprologs zum Corpus des Evangeliums und zu 1 Joh.* Neutestamentliche Abhandlungen, Neue Folge, 20. Münster: Aschendorff, 1988.

Tobin, T. H. *The Creation of Man: Philo and the History of Interpretation.* Washington, D.C.: Catholic Biblical Quarterly Monograph Series 14, 1983.

Weiss, J. *Der erste Korintherbrief.* Göttingen: Vandenhoeck & Ruprecht, 1910.

Welborn, L. L. "Georgi's *Gegner.*" *Journal of Religion* 68 (1988): 566–574.

Wiles, M. "Person or Personification? A Patristic Debate About Logos." In *The Glory of Christ in the New Testament,* ed. L. D. Hurst and N. T. Wright. Oxford: Clarendon Press, 1987, 281–289.

Williams, N. P. *The Ideas of the Fall and of Original Sin.* London: Longmans, 1927.

Index

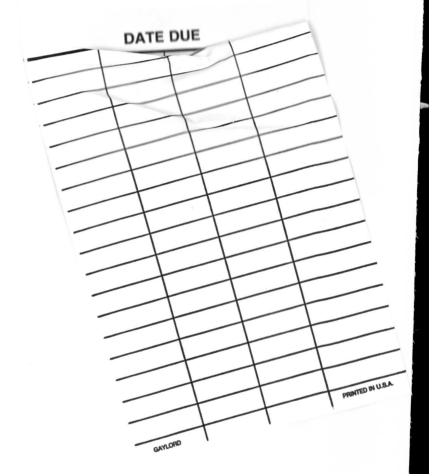

DATE DUE

GAYLORD   PRINTED IN U.S.A.